BORN TO FISH

TIM GALLAGHER and GREG MYERSON

BORN

How an Obsessed Angler

TO

Became the World's Greatest

FISH

Striped Bass Fisherman

Houghton Mifflin Harcourt

Boston   New York   2018

For information about permission to reproduce selections from this book,
write to Permissions, Houghton Mifflin Harcourt Publishing Company,
3 Park Avenue, 19th Floor, New York, New York 10016.

hmhco.com

Library of Congress Cataloging-in-Publication Data
Names: Gallagher, Tim, author. | Myerson, Greg, author.
Title: Born to fish : how an obsessed angler became the world's greatest
striped bass fisherman / Tim Gallagher and Greg Myerson.
Description: Boston : Houghton Mifflin Harcourt, 2018. | Includes
bibliographical references and index.
Identifiers: LCCN 2018005335 (print) | LCCN 2017045339 (ebook) |
ISBN 9780544787452 (ebook) | ISBN 9780544787247 (hardcover : alk. paper)
Subjects: LCSH: Myerson, Greg. | Fishers—Connecticut—Biography. | Bass fishing.
Classification: LCC SH20.M94 (print) | LCC SH20.M94 G35 2018 (ebook) |
DDC 799.17/73092 [B]—dc23
LC record available at https://lccn.loc.gov/2018005335

The names of some of the people portrayed in this book have been changed.

Book design by Greta D. Sibley

Printed in the United States of America
DOC 10 9 8 7 6 5 4 3 2 1

RattleSinker® is a registered trademark of the World Record Striper Company.

CONTENTS

INTRODUCTION

This is the story of a fish — the one most sought after by American anglers for centuries — and a man who has dedicated his life to figuring out what makes this fish tick and how to catch it. And it's the story of the man's great sorrow when he finally landed the largest fish of this species ever caught by a sport fisherman.

The fish is the striped bass, a species that evolved on the eastern coast of North America, breeding in the great bays and estuaries — Chesapeake Bay, Delaware Bay, Long Island Sound, and many huge eastern rivers — and migrating along the Atlantic Coast from northern Maine to the Carolinas. It is a beautiful fish, its streamlined silvery body marked with longitudinal dark stripes from just behind its gills all the way to the base of its tail. Its flesh is tender and succulent, with a slightly sweet taste, making it a popular commercial fish, served in many fine restaurants. It is the state saltwater fish of Maryland, Rhode Island, South Carolina, New York, New Jersey, Virginia, and New Hampshire — and if Congress passes the recently introduced Striped Bass American Heritage Act, it will become the national fish of the United States.

Introduction

The striped bass has earned its status as the "Great American Fish" across the centuries. It was well known to the settlers of the thirteen original colonies, as well as to the Native Americans who preceded them. It was arguably the food source that made it possible for Europeans to gain a foothold in the New World. For the Pilgrims at Plymouth Bay, the striped bass they caught and preserved in salt during the summer got them through the bitterly cold months of their harrowing first winters and allowed their community to survive. The fish were astonishingly numerous then. In his 1637 book, *The New English Canaan*, colonist Thomas Morton wrote, "I my selfe, at the turning of the tyde, have seen such multitudes [of striped bass] passe out . . . that it seemed to mee that one might goe over their backs drishod"—an exaggeration, of course, but a graphic image nonetheless of how common they were. Profits from the sale of striped bass financed the first public school in America in the early 1600s. And America's first conservation law, passed by the Massachusetts Bay Colony in 1639, made it illegal to waste this splendid fish to fertilize crops.

But despite that early conservation effort, striped bass numbers have plummeted, and now millions fewer exist than in colonial times due to overfishing, pollution in the areas they breed, and the decimation of the small fish on which they prey.

The striped bass is easily the most popular saltwater sport fish in the United States—and also hugely popular in the many freshwater lakes and rivers where it has been transplanted. (Like salmon and trout, striped bass can live well in both saltwater and freshwater environments.) It is everyone's fish, attracting the ardor of anglers from the loftiest patricians (United States presidents from George Washington, William Howard Taft, and Theodore Roosevelt to George H. W. and George W. Bush have avidly pursued this fish) to the lowest-paid working-class Americans. Many of them dream of setting a new world record, landing the biggest striped bass ever caught by a sport fisherman. These records don't fall often. A 73-pound striped bass caught in 1913 held the world record until 1982.

Introduction

Catching a world-record striped bass is vastly more important to most anglers than any other fish record. Hardly anyone blinks an eye if someone catches a world-record tuna or marlin, because they can't relate to it. For most people, it is just far too expensive to pursue these big-game fish more than once or twice a year, because it requires special equipment and boats capable of going well away from shore, out to the deep ocean. But you don't even need a boat to fish for stripers. They are available to anyone who lives near the fish's habitat — which includes both coasts of the contiguous United States and many places in between. (The species was successfully introduced to the West Coast in the nineteenth century and later to many lakes and rivers in the interior of the country.) Anyone can buy an inexpensive rod and reel, fish right from the water's edge, and have a chance of landing the biggest striped bass ever caught by a sport fisherman. (The former world-record striped bass, a 78.5-pounder landed by Albert McReynolds in 1982, was caught from a stone jetty on the New Jersey coast.) And people can realistically fish for them every single day if they are so inclined, going out for a couple of hours before or after work. That's why it matters to so many people. It is the people's fish.

This is where the fisherman I mentioned earlier comes in. His name is Greg Myerson, and on August 4, 2011, he caught an 81-pound, 14-ounce female striped bass off the Connecticut coast, shattering a world record that had stood for twenty-nine years.

When world records fall in fishing, some people will say, "Oh, he was just lucky. He happened to be fishing in the right place at the right time." Although that might be true for some records, it certainly isn't for Greg's. He has spent a lifetime figuring out striped bass — observing them closely, studying their behavior, designing revolutionary new lures and fishing techniques — and he knew exactly what he was doing when he caught that fish. Without any training in biological research, he studied the striped bass like a scientist — examining how it hunts, the food it eats, how its behavior is affected by moon phases and the cycles of the tides — at first so he could become a better fisherman but later because the beauty and magnificence of the fish he was pursuing took over his life. Ironically, after he achieved his crowning glory as a striped bass fisherman, breaking the world record, Greg had a staggering epiphany and regretted killing the fish. He had no idea at the time that it might be a world-record fish, and that didn't matter to him. She was a beautiful bass, larger than any he had seen, the kind of fish whose genes should have been passed along to the next generation—and he had killed her just to win a tournament.

Greg has a remarkable backstory, full of challenges he's had to overcome—learning disabilities, substance abuse, extreme violence (done to him and by him), a father who was in the mob. And he has done more than just overcome: he has triumphed.

At forty-nine years old, Greg is a big man, with close-cropped, ginger-colored hair and a goatee, who perpetually wears a cap, indoors and out. Standing six feet, four inches tall and weighing more than 275 pounds, he towers over most people. In college, at the University of Rhode Island, he was a Division I linebacker, and he looks the part. He went there on a full athletic scholarship, but he could easily have gotten a free ride at any of the top football colleges in America, several of which aggressively attempted to recruit him. He chose URI because of its immediate proximity to great striped bass fishing.

Looking at Greg, you know he would have no qualms about taking on anyone in a fight—and indeed, when he was younger he would get into huge brawls, sometimes clearing out bars single-handedly. He never started the fights, but it didn't take much to set him off. He carried a rage inside that could explode at any moment, and men who made the mistake of crossing him in those days often ended up unconscious outside the bar. That's hard to imagine now, since he seems so good-natured and easygoing. And yet you know it's there, like a volcano waiting to erupt, and you don't want to be there when it happens.

Greg's fishing is the only thing that's allowed him to cope with all the pressures and frustrations of his life through the years. Whenever things have gotten unbearably bad, he has hit the water to escape whatever problems he faced on land. It has always been like a tonic and a pressure-release valve for him, and he could not have survived without it.

AT THE TURNING
OF THE TIDE

It is already well past sundown as we leave the shelter of Westbrook Harbor, but the rising moon, golden orange on this warm August evening, casts an eerie glow over Long Island Sound, giving the water the sheen of burnished copper. Out in the open now, Greg pushes the boat's throttle forward, and we slice easily through the flat-calm sea. It is so peaceful here, so different from the pulsing grind of the city whose lights twinkle just a few miles away. Except for a handful of small sportfishing boats scattered over this vast expanse of water, we are alone.

It was on a night like this in 2011 that Greg caught the largest striped bass ever landed by a sport fisherman, smashing a world record that had stood for nearly three decades. He knew it was a huge fish the instant he jerked up on the rod to set the hook deep in her mouth, before she took off, swimming powerfully against the current and towing the boat behind her. But we don't talk about any of that tonight. This is my first fishing trip with Greg, and I'm eager to see him in action and learn from him.

Greg knows right where he's going—a submerged outcropping of rocky crags, some thirty feet below the surface, where sea life thrives:

crabs, lobsters, bluefish, but above all, striped bass. He has made this trip well over a thousand times since he first came here as a ten-year-old, unbeknownst to his parents, powering his tiny skiff well beyond all bounds of safety and common sense, braving the most dangerous and treacherous tides. He has always been unstoppable when he sets his mind to something.

Greg has spent a lifetime figuring the striped bass out, like a scientist puzzling over a problem, trying to develop a working hypothesis: What do these fish want? How can I catch more of them? How can I entice the biggest of them to take the bait?

As we near the submerged rocks, he backs the throttle down to an idle, and we drift freely with the tidal surge. It's time to pull the fishing rods from the rack and rig up. Greg grabs a rag from the deck and uses it to hold on to a slippery live eel he has pulled from the bait tank. Raising the squirming eel above him, he brings it down sharply, striking its head against the gunwale with a resounding *thwack*, knocking it senseless. He then carefully forces a fishhook through its tough hide, just behind its head. Dangling about a foot below the fishhook is one of Greg's RattleSinkers, designed to mimic the sound of a lobster's carapace as it scuttles along the rocks. Greg spent many years figuring out that big striped bass love to eat lobsters and how to exploit that fact. It's a classic bait-and-switch scheme: the bass hears the sound from perhaps fifty feet away and swims over, expecting to find a lobster. Then it smells the eel and takes that instead. It is especially effective on a night like this, in late summer, under a glowing quarter-moon, at the turning of the tide. It has certainly worked for Greg, who has caught more large striped bass than any sport fisherman in history.

All set now, with rods and bait ready, Greg throttles up again, pushing the boat against the current, moving well upstream of the submerged rocks, then kills the motor. The silence is startling: the only sound is the whisper of a gentle breeze as we drift with the flow. Greg is a picture of concentration, almost like a conductor, controlling every action in the orchestra. He tells me exactly what to do: hold the rod pointing at a downward angle; grip it loosely with my left hand while the fingers of my other hand rest lightly on the butt of the rod, sensitive to the slightest movement in the water below. I let out line until the sinker hits the rocks, then reel up about a foot so the eel dangles slightly above them as we drift.

The rocks are invisible below us, but Greg knows right where we are. "About twenty seconds," he says. The depth of his concentration is palpable. "The fish is going to hit . . . right . . . *now!*" And simultaneously with his last word a striped bass slams into my eel. (This scenario is repeated again and again throughout the evening.) I lift up firmly on the rod tip, setting the hook, and the fight is on, the rod bending wildly as the fish strips out line, trying to escape. But the hook and line hold, and I soon bring the fish alongside. Greg scoops a big landing net under it and pulls it out of the water briefly. The fish is about a yard long and probably weighs close to twenty pounds—not a huge bass, and certainly nothing like the fish Greg routinely hauls in, but it's nice to start the evening with some action. I quickly remove the hook, and Greg lowers the bass into the water again, where it revives instantly and goes shooting away from us, no doubt glad to be back in its watery domain.

In the course of the evening, I catch a couple more decent fish, but I miss others, striking an instant too soon or too late when the bass hit my eel. But Greg never misses. He seems to haul in striped bass at will, and they are all larger than any I catch.

I've been an avid fisherman for most of my life, and I've known many people I would rank as experts in the art and craft of angling, but Greg is something else entirely. I knew on this first fishing trip with him that I was in the presence of a master, or even more than that. Greg is the Mozart of fishermen—and perhaps I am like Antonio Salieri, able to recognize his genius, the seemingly effortless brilliance and creativity of his pursuit for fish, but unable to accomplish anything meaningful as a fisherman myself. In his presence, I feel like a complete novice. It is both inspiring and depressing.

But this is not just a story about Greg Myerson. It's about a fish, a way of life, and the fate of our oceans. What is it about the striped bass? Why do so many people pursue this fish with such unbridled ardor, forsaking sleep for days on end during the fish's migration, driving the beaches endlessly, searching for the telltale signs of bass chasing small fish to the surface and attacking them ferociously in the gleaming light of a harvest moon? It is a fascination almost primordial in its intensity: the hunter staring longingly to sea, hoping to do battle with mythical leviathans. And striped bass *are* rugged battlers. In the violent rip currents between ocean and shore they emerge, slashing and diving in the churning cauldron of bubbling water, where the sea pounds hard against the rocky shore.

Greg has been there thousands of times. For him and other avid striped bass anglers, this is more a lifestyle than a sport. They live to catch this fish. It occupies their minds round the clock, especially when the fish are migrating along the coast. More than a few East Coast anglers wake in the night when the fish are moving through and hit the beaches, standing in waist-deep water at the edge of the rolling surf with rods more than ten feet long, pitching bait or flies, or lures with names like Ballistic Missile and Atom Striper Swiper, hoping to hook into a striped bass. Or they trudge to the end of a long, slippery rock jetty, or head out in boats, large and small, oblivious to the time as the rest of the world sleeps. They become experts on the tides and the phases of the moon. They are nothing if not passionate.

And that is exactly the dilemma: too many people want to catch striped bass—the larger the better—and all too many of the fish end up dead, including a lot of the large females (called *cows* by anglers), which are just the kind of fish whose genes should be passed on to the next generation to ensure the quality of the breeding stock.

One of the things about Greg Myerson that interested me most when I first met him six years ago was his deep concern for the fish he was catching. Here he had worked his entire life to become the top striped bass fisherman in the world, and just when he achieved this crowning goal, he had misgivings. He decided to step back from what he was doing and think about what was best for the striped bass themselves. Although he still fishes almost every day of bass season, he has turned away from killing big bass and wants no part anymore in tournaments that kill them. Greg is now actively promoting catch-and-release tournaments. On his Facebook page, he often states how long it has been since he caused the death of a striped bass—currently more than three years.

You may well wonder where a person like Greg Myerson came from: what factors in his background came together to produce such a competent and thoroughly obsessive angler. This is what I hope to provide in the pages of this book, an intimate look at the making of a world-champion fisherman—a man who was born to fish.

BORN TO FISH

Herb Myerson could not have been more different from his son Greg. Although they were both strong and athletic, Herb had always been a city boy. Raised in Brooklyn, he'd never known any other life but the dense urban sprawl of New York, whereas from his earliest days, Greg loved nature and being out in the country.

Everybody loved Herb. Outgoing and charismatic, he stood six foot three and weighed 260 pounds, but he was lithe and graceful and enjoyed dancing. Tanned, handsome, and muscular, with thick, jet-black hair, he had once modeled shirts for magazine ads. But that wasn't surprising: he came from a family of good-looking people. Herb's aunt was Bess Myerson, who had won the Miss America pageant in 1945 and been a popular television personality in the 1950s and '60s.

Herb was a Vietnam vet and had moved into his parents' apartment in Hamden, Connecticut, when he first returned from the war. It was there, at a party, that he met Diane, a beautiful young widow who lived in the same building with her one-year-old son, David. Her husband had become seriously ill and passed away a short time earlier. She and Herb were immediately drawn to each other and made a striking couple. They often went dancing and also loved to go bowling. But the two had very different temperaments. Herb was the picture of cool. Beyond unflappable, nothing got to him, but his calm could be frightening at times. Diane was the opposite, volatile and emotional, always ready to explode. But they soon got married, and a couple of years later, Greg was born.

Herb adopted David and made him a Myerson. Neither Greg nor David knew they were half brothers until they were grown up. They had no reason to wonder. They looked alike—tall, strong, and athletic—and spoke in a similar way. And Herb and the rest of his family treated the two boys exactly the same. There was never any favoritism. Herb was the only father Dave ever knew, and Herb completely embraced him.

The Myerson family had an interesting religious mix—Diane was from a devout Polish Catholic family, and Herb's family was Jewish. They observed the important sacred holidays of both faiths, celebrating Christmas and Hanukkah, Easter and Passover. Although Herb was more of a secular Jew, his father was devout, regularly attending synagogue and making sure Greg and Dave observed Hanukkah and other major religious events in the Jewish calendar.

Greg was only a toddler when his family moved from their apartment in downtown Hamden into a Colonial-style house they had built in a rural area, with woods and farmland, near North Haven, which proved an ideal home for Greg and Dave. From the start, Greg lived to be outdoors, close to nature. He had no interest in the pursuits of his family and most other people his age.

Herb and Diane never understood Greg's ways—his constant need to be roaming the woods and fields and streams near their home. They knew only urban life. But Greg was a remarkable child who followed his own path from his earliest days. And he was always obsessed with fishing. Even as a two-year-old, he would stand for hours with his toy fishing rod, dangling a plastic fishhook into the muddy water of the drainage ditch in front of his house. Aunt Cookie, Diane's youngest sister, told me no one could drag him away from that ditch.

"He would sit there for hours every day, loving it," she said. Later he started building dams with stones in the tiny stream that flowed through his backyard, and he'd catch the little fish he found there, mostly shiners.

"I was always there," said Greg. "I loved it."

Greg was like a latter-day Huck Finn—but where did that come from? He seemed like such an anomaly in his family and in the town where he grew up. His high school football coach, Phil Ottochian, perhaps put it best: "He was born in the wrong century," he told me, laughing. "He should have been a pioneer—*The Plainsman*."

Where Greg got his obsession with fishing, nobody knows. His parents certainly didn't encourage it. They had no interest in field sports or any kind of nature-related activities. But he did get some encouragement from outside his immediate family. His grandmother's backyard was right on the Muddy River in North Haven, and his Aunt Cookie was always fascinated by Greg's overpowering interest in fishing. She recalls sitting with her mother on lawn chairs at the edge of the river and watching young Greg trying to fish as a four-year-old. His preoccupation with fishing was good for Cookie and her mother because it gave them time to talk with each other instead of spending all their time looking after Greg. One day, Greg was getting discouraged because he hadn't gotten any bites. "You just need to keep trying, Gregory," said his grandmother. "It takes a lot of patience to catch a fish." Another two hours passed, still with no action. He finally dropped his rod to the ground. "I don't think there's any fishies in here, Grammy," he told her.

Greg's mother always had to insist that Greg be allowed to take a fishing rod to various summer camps or on vacation with them or he would refuse to go. Going to Florida as a kid, he wouldn't even get in the car unless they either brought a fishing rod or promised that his Uncle Donny would have one for him when they got there.

"A fishing rod has been a part of me, like an attachment to my body, for most of my life," said Greg. "When I was a kid, walking up and down the streets, I always had one."

Seymour Myerson, Greg's grandfather, encouraged his interest in fishing. A big, good-looking man much like his son Herb, Seymour was also very good-natured; he enjoyed spending time with Greg. Although he knew nothing about fishing himself—his only connection to it was that he had once worked in the Fulton Fish Market in Brooklyn—he could see Greg loved it, so he started looking for places to take him. When Greg was still in nursery school, but already a decent young angler, Seymour found a place called Corey's Fish Farm not far from Greg's house, and he started taking him there whenever he came to visit. It was one of those places where you pay by the pound for any trout you catch, and some of them were good sized. The place had three ponds—two were about a half-acre in size and the other was more of a lake—with a shack in between. The smaller ponds each had a huge fountain in the middle, shooting water high in the air, to keep it aerated. Corey lived in the shack and had big mounted trout hanging on the walls.

"I loved that place," said Greg. "I would stare at those mounted trout like they were the greatest things in the world—and to me, they were."

He would stand at the edge of the pond for hours, casting his baited hook as far as he could. Mr. Corey took a liking to Greg and showed him how to fish more effectively for the trout—by forming trout meal into a ball around the fishhook. This was what they fed the trout every day, so it was amazingly effective.

"After a while, I became a regular at Corey's, and he didn't charge me to fish," said Greg. "I would help out, feeding the fish and cleaning up." He and Corey would talk for hours about trout. And Greg loved bringing home the fish he caught to his family. He would also take trout to his nursery school teacher. Greg always insisted on giving trout to Seymour, who didn't really like to eat fish but took them anyway to avoid upsetting Greg, thanking him profusely and then tossing them out his car window into the woods a half-mile down the road. (One day a policeman saw him do this and pulled him over for littering. But he had to laugh when Seymour explained the situation, and he let him go with a warning.)

Before he was even kindergarten age, Greg had his first close brush with death after being stung repeatedly by a swarm of yellow jackets. He'd stirred up the wasps by poking a hockey stick into their underground nest. He had an intense allergic reaction to the stings and went into anaphylactic shock. (Before this, no one had known he was allergic to the stings of bees, wasps, and hornets.) Within seconds, he fell to the ground, barely able to breathe. He managed to crawl into the kitchen and collapsed in front of his mother, who was having coffee with a neighbor. In a panic, his mother called the paramedics, and shortly after they arrived, an ambulance rushed him to the nearest hospital. Greg remembers being put on a stretcher and looking up at the paramedics as they ran toward the ambulance and rushed him inside, his mind hovering at the edge of unconsciousness. He didn't feel fear at this point, but almost a sense of fascination with the rapid events unfolding around him as he lay dazed and fading on the stretcher.

For the paramedics, it was a frantic race. Greg needed equipment that only the hospital had to keep him breathing and stabilize him. His lungs had collapsed by the time he entered the emergency room; his condition was so grave that a priest was brought in to administer last rites. By then, Greg had already slipped into a coma. When he finally awoke days later, most of Greg's family were gathered in his hospital room. Seymour stood next to his bed, smiling broadly and tearfully as Greg opened his eyes. The sense of relief Seymour, Herb, and Diane felt when Greg awoke, after days of languishing in a coma, was so profound they all burst out laughing.

"I remember waking up and seeing my grandfather standing there laughing," said Greg. "They were all laughing."

GREG'S MOTHER taught history at Norwalk High School, having earned her master's degree at Quinnipiac College. Diane always pushed her sons academically, determined that they would be successful and lead meaningful lives. But her pushiness irked Greg from a very young age. Although he was always a bright child, he was dyslexic, so reading did not come easily to him.

"My mother and I really never got along," said Greg. "She was always preaching at me, trying to teach me things. We would butt heads all the time; I never wanted to listen to her."

Greg began staying frequently at Diane's mother's home. She lived in a tiny house with her ninety-nine-year-old father, right on the banks of the Muddy River, about four miles away. Quiet and self-effacing, she was nothing like Diane, and Greg loved to spend time with her.

Greg's great-grandfather, who spoke only Polish, had his own room in the house. He and his relatives had come to America in the heyday of Ellis Island, when thousands of immigrants flooded into the United States. The family brought a strong work ethic and a need to lead purposeful lives, ever pushing to improve their lot. They had bought a huge house in New Haven early in the twentieth century, and all of their relatives who moved to America would live in it until they got on their feet and could afford their own homes. Theirs was a culture of always striving to improve, to become the best you could hope to be. This is the ethic Diane had inherited and perhaps the reason she often seemed unbearably pushy, especially to Greg, causing him to flee to her mother's home so often.

Greg would spend hours there watching Red Sox games on television with his great-grandfather, who would always wear a Red Sox cap and smoke his pipe. "Just about the only word he said that I recognized was 'Yastrzemski,'" said Greg, laughing. "He'd say, 'Yastrzemski go three round!' which meant Carl Yastrzemski had just hit a triple." After his great-grandfather died, Greg moved into his room and lived with his grandmother for months. She was a devout Catholic and would pray the rosary each morning when it was quiet. "I would sit there on the couch and do it with her," said Greg. "I loved it."

When Greg was six years old, the family went to visit his father's relatives in Florida. His Uncle Donny owned a textile factory there and had a sport-fishing boat he kept at a yacht club in the Florida Keys. One day they were having a big party on the boat and everyone was drinking cocktails and eating shrimp. As always, Greg had brought a fishing rod with him, so he grabbed a few shrimp to use as bait and walked down to the end of the dock. After baiting his hook, he cast it out into the water and began reeling in. Then he spotted a huge barracuda, nearly six feet long, and cast the shrimp right in front of it. The barracuda attacked instantly, grabbing the shrimp with a huge splash. It took off so fast and powerfully, it ripped the rod right out of Greg's hands, and he fell off the end of the dock. He panicked, splashing and crying until his uncle and parents came running up and rescued him.

"What the hell happened?" asked Uncle Donny.

"A big long fish took my rod," said Greg. His uncle quickly hired a diver to go under the dock and retrieve the lost fishing rod.

"My Uncle Donny was a really bad dude," Greg told me. "He was my dad's sister's husband. He used to call me the Cop Killer when I was a little kid. He hated cops because he was a criminal. He had me convinced that I'd killed a cop. I was terrified, because whenever a cop car came by, he'd pretend they were after me, and I would hide. When you're a little kid and someone says you did something, you believe it. My parents would laugh about it and think it was funny. My mother would say, 'Oh, don't do that to him.' But I was terrified. He always called me the Cop Killer, and I hated it."

A short time after they returned from Florida, Greg's family joined the beach club at Branford Harbor, and they spent every weekend at the shoreline, so he grew up always being near the ocean. They would often eat lunch at a restaurant overlooking Long Island Sound. One day he watched some fishermen in a boat just offshore, catching bluefish one after another. He was completely enthralled.

"My parents kept yelling at me to eat, but I just kept staring out the window, watching these guys fish," said Greg. "I thought it was the greatest thing in the world, and I knew right then and there that I had to have my own boat someday."

Greg had a hard time learning during his early years in elementary school. In addition to having dyslexia, which made reading difficult, he probably had obsessive-compulsive disorder and attention deficit hyperactivity disorder, though the latter two conditions were not diagnosed at the time. He couldn't concentrate at all on his work in class and constantly daydreamed—usually about fishing. Even just walking around school could present problems for him. For one thing, he always felt a powerful need to step up onto a curb or a staircase with his right foot first, so it stressed him whenever he was approaching them as he tried to estimate the distance in his mind and shorten or lengthen his stride so his right foot would be in the correct position to step up when he got there.

"It drove me crazy," said Greg. "It was starting to get really noticeable, and I felt like I had to hide it from everybody."

Greg's dyslexia was diagnosed when he was in third grade, and he started taking special education classes to help him with his reading and math skills. The classes were useful, and he attended them for several years. He especially appreciated the efforts of Miss Flynn, one of the two special ed teachers at the school. All three of the boys she was working with—especially Greg—loved to go fishing, so she tried to incorporate fishing into their lessons so they would pay attention. (One of the other kids in the program was Scott Jackson, who became a lifelong friend of Greg's.)

"The things we read and the math problems she gave us were almost always about fishing," said Greg. "Like, 'If you catch this many fish and you do this, how many fish will you have?' It was great."

The downside was that Greg and the other two boys were the only students in the entire school taking these classes, so it set them apart from their schoolmates. Everyone knew what was happening when Greg would get called out of his regular class to go to special ed, and his classmates made fun of him. He became hyperaware of his disabilities, which gave him a sense of inadequacy in some areas of his day-to-day life.

But in fishing he knew he was absolutely capable—the most capable person around—and it became his escape from everything in his life that made him feel bad: his learning disabilities, his often testy relationship with his mother, and bullying by his classmates. At the edge of the water, his concentration was absolute as he closed his eyes and imagined the fish swimming underwater somewhere right before him. He was always trying to put himself into their minds, obsessively striving to understand everything about them. The rest of the world just melted away. He had found the essence of his being: to be a fisherman. Nothing else mattered.

GREG WAS somewhat of a nerd in elementary school, always doing his obsessive experiments—burning ants with a magnifying glass; collecting bugs; drawing underwater scenes of trout, bass, and other fish. It drove many of his teachers to distraction, except one.

"I remember one of my teachers, Mr. Mondillo, saw me drawing this beautiful freshwater fish scene when I was supposed to be working on a project," said Greg.

"Wow, that's pretty good," said Mr. Mondillo.

"Thanks!"

"But that's not what you're supposed to be working on."

"I know, but that's all I can think about."

"Well, I can understand that. I fish too."

"Really?" Greg was amazed to find out he had a teacher who shared his interest in fishing.

Just a few days later, Greg was fishing at a nearby lake when he ran into Mr. Mondillo and another teacher fishing there. They weren't catching anything, so Greg gave them a few pointers, and they caught a couple of pan fish. Then he asked them if they wanted to try fishing at a really great place, and they eagerly agreed. To reach the site, a pond on the far side of a farm, he took them a roundabout way, hiking on a muddy trail through the woods. He neglected to tell them it was private property and they were trespassing.

The fishing was fabulous, and they hauled in one largemouth bass after another, having the time of their lives. "This is really great, Greg!" said Mr. Mondillo.

Greg smiled and started to cast his lure again when suddenly he noticed the farmer walk out the back door of his house. "Run!" he screamed at the teachers.

"Why?" asked Mr. Mondillo, but Greg was already racing away through the woods.

"They started running with me, these two older teachers," said Greg. "And they're like, 'What the fuck?' I said, 'You can't fish here.' It was funny as hell. I'd sneak into this pond, and the farmer would chase me out all the time. My teachers busted my chops about it later, but I know they loved it."

Each year, a huge fair took place at North Haven, featuring roller coasters, shooting galleries, baseball tosses, and other attractions, as well as numerous booths. Greg's favorite was the trout club booth, where you could learn to tie flies. He never got past that booth when he went to the fair with his father and his brother. The man showed him step-by-step how to tie a fly, using feathers, thread, and model cement. The first time this happened, Herb and Dave just left him there and went off in search of carnival rides. When they returned hours later, Greg was still completely engrossed in tying flies and had no interest whatsoever in going on rides, eating cotton candy, or other fair staples. That first year at the fair, he came back to the trout booth four days in a row and became a proficient fly tyer. He was seven years old.

Not long after this, his paternal grandmother's parrot died. She was devastated by the death of her bird, so Greg comforted her and offered to bury it—but first he pulled out a few clumps of its feathers to use for tying trout flies. The parrot feathers were a gaudy green and yellow and made a fly that really stood out—which came in handy the day he first tried out one of the flies on a nearby river. The water was high and muddy from a recent storm, making visibility poor for the fish. But a huge sea-run rainbow trout, still glistening chromelike from its time in the ocean, hammered the fly, and the fight was on. Greg's cheap fly rod was barely a match for this mighty fish as it surged away, making run after run as it fought to escape, bending the rod double, but Greg finally managed to land the trout and put it on a stringer.

Herb happened to drive down to the river that day, looking for his son, and asked him if he was catching anything. His mouth dropped when Greg pulled the stringer from the water and showed him the enormous trout, more than twenty inches long. The next day, the front page of the local newspaper featured a picture of Greg wearing a crimson Boston Red Sox hat and grinning widely as he held up his prized fish.

The yard at the Myerson house was big enough to serve as a football or baseball field for local kids, and they would sometimes have huge neighborhood games there. Greg's brother Dave was the star even then. He would often get Greg to stand at a makeshift home plate in front of a wooden fence while he threw sizzling fastballs and curve balls at him.

"The fence was all pushed in from him throwing fastballs at me," said Greg. "I'd be crying, but Dave wouldn't let me stop. I grew up playing sports with him and his friends, who were always at least two or three years older than me."

It was cruel, but it made Greg into a phenomenal slugger. "I wound up becoming a really good hitter, because he'd be throwing these hundred-mile-an-hour fastballs and curve balls and all this other crap at me. And sometimes he would bean me—on purpose. So when I got to Little League, I led the team and league in home runs all the time. The pitches that I saw in Little League were a hell of a lot slower than what he was throwing."

Dave was always the star, and he quickly advanced from Little League to the Babe Ruth League, a prestigious international baseball program. The Babe Ruth field was next to the Little League field, separated by a wire fence. Greg, a lefty, would often hit home runs high over the fence, and the ball would bounce right in the middle of the Babe

Ruth field as Dave stood at the pitcher's mound. "Dave would always give me the thumbs-up as I was jogging around the bases."

Verne Carlson was the same age as Greg and lived just down the street from him. They were both avid anglers in elementary school and were trout fishing on a nearby river the first time they met, Greg using dry flies and Verne bait-fishing with worms. Verne bet him he'd catch more trout using bait than Greg would with flies, so the race was on. They were both very competitive and fished hard, up and down the river, catching fish after fish, but at the end of the day Greg had won handily.

"After that, we would go trudging together up the river for miles all the time, catching rainbows, browns, and brook trout," said Greg. "We'd fish every spot we could find, walking all the way from North Haven to the MacKenzie Reservoir in Wallingford, going through the woods, then breaking out into where the river went through farmland. We caught a lot of trout back then and released most of them."

Verne's father was one of the most over-the-top anglers Greg had ever met. He was absolutely obsessed with catching striped bass, a fish Greg had not yet ever caught—*and* he owned a boat. Mr. Carlson ran a family business installing wood floors in houses throughout the area. He was strong and muscular from the work and bore a striking resemblance to Sheriff Andy Taylor of *The Andy Griffith Show*, which Greg enjoyed watching as a kid. He usually dressed in a T-shirt and blue jeans, as he had probably been doing since he was in his teens in the mid-1950s.

The first time Mr. Carlson took Greg on one of their fishing trips, they went far out into Long Island Sound, all the way to the Race, at the far eastern edge of the sound, where it meets the Atlantic Ocean—a place of turbulent crosscurrents, powerful riptides, and surging seas. It was as if a whole new world had opened up for Greg, full of adventure and a sense of freedom as the boat rocketed across the pounding sea, splashing salt spray over them as they motored through powerful swells and wind chop.

It was there, within sight of the Race Rock lighthouse, that Greg hooked his first striped bass. The power of the fish shocked him, instantly bending his fishing rod double, lifting him off his feet, and almost pulling him over the side. Mr. Carlson quickly grabbed him by the back of his pants with one hand. He was already holding Verne, who'd hooked another equally large fish.

"Keep reeling!" shouted Mr. Carlson. "Don't let go of those rods!"

"We were both literally coming up off the deck with the rods in our hands, fighting those fish," said Greg. "It was the most exciting thing ever. Mr. Carlson was a very strong guy. The fish would definitely have pulled us right over the side if he wasn't holding the two of us by our belts."

The sense of accomplishment Greg felt when he finally brought the fish alongside and Mr. Carlson helped him haul it aboard was indescribable. Nearly forty inches long, the striper weighed close to thirty pounds. And it was beautiful, the most stunning fish Greg had ever seen: sleek, silvery white, and strikingly marked with bold black lines running from its gills to its tail. Although he was exhausted, and the muscles in his arms burned so much from the intensity of his effort that he could barely lift them, he couldn't wait to pick up his rod, bait the hook with a fresh eel, and get ready for the next tidal drift.

"Oh my God, I was in love with it!" said Greg. "I just wanted to catch them again and again."

The three of them caught several more stripers that day, each one just as exciting for Greg to fight as the first one. He was absolutely hooked by striped bass fishing, by everything about it—the beauty of the fish, the ferocity of their fight to escape, and the places where you went to catch them. This was his first real taste of going out to sea in a boat to pursue fish, and he loved it. He was still in awe as they motored back to the harbor on the way home, and he tried to memorize the route they had taken and the places they'd fished. He knew he'd be returning here again—by himself if necessary.

Over the years, the vast and often turbulent waters of Long Island Sound would become a refuge to Greg, a place where he could escape the many cares he had back on land—his difficulties with schoolwork, his disabilities, his mother's constant nagging. Although he was not quite eight years old, his single-mindedness was astounding even then. He started saving coins in a coffee can and doing whatever he could to earn money: catching baitfish to sell to fishermen; planting tomatoes for a nearby farmer; doing odd jobs for anyone who had some extra chores he could do. And always, his goal of one day having his own motorboat, so he could go out into Long Island Sound anytime he wanted, kept him going.

MARRIED TO THE MOB

Greg's family led a strange life, due partly to Herb's endless ambition. Right out of the service he had gotten into the liquor business, running package stores. Then he became a bookie for a crime family—which must have been a shock to Diane, the high school teacher, but apparently the money and lifestyle the mob provided was too attractive to pass up, and she looked the other way.

Greg's brother, Dave, explained it this way: "I think she just pretended it didn't exist," he said. "She knew it was there, and there were just pure logistics like you've got phone calls coming in. He used to have these little monitors on the phone, and he would say that if the red light came on, hang up the phone, because someone was tapping the line. So it was really obvious to everyone what was going on, but it wasn't something that my mom talked about—ever."

Herb would often host huge parties at their house, which was perfect for the purpose—large, isolated, and difficult for the police or FBI to watch. Often thirty or more people would show up, various mobsters and their girlfriends. Diane would stop the men at the door and make them hand over their pistols before they could come inside. She'd pile the guns in a fruit bowl beside the front door and give them back when they left. Most of the men who came to Herb's parties were absurdly stereotypical mobster types, both funny and terrifying—big, dark, pushy Italian American mugs, with names like Frankie Potatoes and Joey Fingers, speaking in working-class New York accents. They would have loud, raucous poker games, sitting around the table together, cussing, smoking cigars, and sometimes getting into fistfights with each other, while their girlfriends lounged beside the swimming pool. Sometimes it got so bad, Diane would scream at them: "Look, I've got kids in the house. If you're going to play cards here, no guns, no fights, no bad language!"

Greg hated the parties. "I was a quiet kid," he said. "I didn't want any part of that. I was usually downstairs in the basement, tying flies to take fishing. When they would fight and yell and scream playing poker, it hurt my ears. I was like a country hillbilly living with all these mobsters," he said, laughing.

Some of the goons who frequented Herb's parties took a liking to Greg. He remembers two in particular named Al and Sal who seemed so interchangeable he could barely remember who was who, except that Al had a goofier personality. Both had mustaches and black hair, stood more than six feet tall, and easily weighed 300 pounds. They were scary men, but always friendly to Greg. Sometimes they'd drop by the house when Diane wasn't home and let Greg shoot their pistols in the backyard, blowing gaping holes in tin cans or blasting Coke bottles into oblivion. Then they'd hand Greg a twenty-dollar bill and say, "Go spend this someplace."

Once when an elementary school friend of Greg's was visiting him at his house while his parents were away, they found one of Herb's pistols in a drawer.

"Do you think it's loaded?" his friend asked.

"Naw, I don't think so," said Greg. Then he pulled the trigger, blowing a hole through several walls of the house, the bullet finally stopping in a book on a shelf in his parents' bedroom. Greg desperately squeezed white toothpaste into the holes, trying to hide where the bullet had gone through.

Although Herb was Jewish, he became a vital member of the Italian crime family he was associated with. It was often Herb who set the odds on football games and other sporting events for the syndicate, and he was good at it. He made a great deal of money for the mob and became powerful in his own right.

Herb was never violent at home—he was the opposite; nothing made him lose his cool with his wife and kids. But Greg remembers a couple of times when he blew up at people who crossed him. One day, just as the family sat down for dinner, a man who owed Herb a large amount of money showed up at the front door.

"He had a bunch of pot, big bags of weed, to try to pay my father off, right in front of me and my brother and mother," said Greg.

Herb exploded. He grabbed the man and threw him outside. Then, lifting him up from the ground, he punched him again and again till he lay unconscious on the driveway.

"He finally came back in the house, acting like nothing had happened, and started eating dinner," said Greg.

Another time, just after Greg started junior high school, Herb gave him some pointers on how to take care of himself in a street fight. A couple of the toughest kids at school had taken a bitter dislike to Greg and were making his life miserable. They were brothers and rode on the school bus with him every day. The two picked on him at every opportunity. One day they cornered him in a school restroom. As the larger brother held Greg firmly in a bear hug, the other took a deep draw from a cigarette and held it with the bright ember aglow right next to Greg's eyes, threatening to blind him. He burned Greg's face repeatedly as Greg struggled to escape.

"We were at the dinner table that night, and I had all these burn marks around my eyes," Greg told me. His father noticed immediately.

"What the hell happened to your face?" he asked. Greg looked down, silent. "Those are burns . . . cigarette burns," said Herb, aghast. "Someone stuck a fucking cigarette in your face!" he said, becoming more and more steamed.

Greg finally admitted what had happened, and his father insisted he give him all the details. "It was the Allen brothers," said Greg. Herb knew all about them and about their father—a low-level drug dealer and gangster wannabe, nicknamed "Big Daddy Car" because he always drove around in a big red Cadillac.

As he listened, the redness left Herb's face, and a scary coolness descended over him. "This is what you got to do," he said. "When the school bus drops you off tomorrow, be sure to get off first, then wait at the bottom of the steps. When the first kid gets off the bus, punch him in the throat as hard as you can." Greg grimaced and glanced downward. Herb grabbed Greg's shoulder and looked him in the eyes. "I mean it. Don't punch him in the head; punch him in the throat. Then you can fight one-on-one with the other kid."

As the bus left the school the next afternoon, Greg was sitting in the front, near the driver. He glanced to the back and saw that the brothers were not sitting together. The smaller of the two was closer to the front of the bus, but they were both much bigger than Greg. As Greg got off the bus, he turned to one side and waited as everyone exited and walked past him. The instant the boy stepped off the bus, Greg landed a devastating blow to his throat, and he fell like a puppet with its strings cut, lying on the ground, choking and completely incapacitated. The boy's brother saw everything and began forcing his way to the front of the bus, throwing other students out of his way as he raced to get outside. Greg tried to run, but the boy chased him down, tackling him to the ground. He smashed Greg's head again and again against the concrete curb until he was bleeding profusely from his face.

Herb took one look at Greg when he got home and told him to get in the car. He drove straight to Big Daddy Car's house and rang the doorbell as Greg sat in the passenger seat of the car. When the man opened his front door, Herb took him by the collar and dragged him outside.

"Look what your goddamn kids did to my son!" he shouted, pointing at Greg. He grabbed the man by the back of his head and slammed his face into the hood of his car again and again until he dropped to the ground, unconscious and covered with blood, then kicked him out of the way like a sack of garbage. Herb got into the car, and he and Greg rode silently all the way home.

I spoke with Greg's older brother, Dave, about what it was like growing up with a mob-connected father, and he told me about another time he'd seen Herb snap, after he rear-ended a car. "The person in front stopped, and my dad hit him," said Dave. "Not badly, but he just bumped right into him. The guy got out and was all pissed off. I remember my dad grabbing this guy and throwing him across the front of his car—like he can hit you, and then it's your fault."

Other unspeakably violent events took place in Herb's world. The day after Herb sold one of his liquor stores, the man who bought it was thrown down a flight of stairs and shot five times.

"I don't know what the hell happened, or if my father had anything to do with it," said Greg. "He owned a bunch of liquor stores, and he sold one to this guy. Maybe he pissed him off or something. I'd seen my father in action. He really had a temper. He was usually nice—but if you got him pissed off . . ."

But Herb was not all bad. He was a mass of contradictions—a mix of Tony Soprano and Mike Brady. And he hung around at home all day like Ozzie Nelson.

"He was always locked in his upstairs office all day Saturday and Sunday," said Dave. "It was always calls coming in, calls going out. He was basically running the whole book."

Dave particularly remembers one time when he was very young and was going with his father to a breakfast at the Knights of Columbus hall. "When we were walking out he tells me, 'Look up at that third-story window in the building across the street. Smile, the FBI's taking your picture.' And apparently they really were. I never connected the dots as a kid. It was just normal. We always had lots of uncles, who weren't really uncles; folks who were coming over all the time."

Once when he was in high school, Dave was unknowingly dating the daughter of a major crime boss. One day, three tough-looking men confronted him.

"Do you know who her dad is?" one of them asked.

"Yeah, I met him," said Dave. "I think he runs some kind of paper business or something."

"No! He's the big dude," the man said, looking Dave hard in the eyes. "Do not screw this up."

"I had no idea I was dating Meadow Soprano," Dave told me, laughing.

Herb always drove Cadillac Sevilles that were either gray or black. One of Dave's early memories was his dad driving him to Little League practice one day, and he had to sit in the middle of the front seat because there were several other people in the car. He felt something hard on the seat under him, covered by a blanket. Dave reached down and pulled out a pistol. "You've got to move this gun, Dad, because I can't sit down," he told him.

"But honestly, I just never even thought about it," said Dave. "It was just the way we lived. The funny thing is, my dad was a super nice guy, the nicest guy in the world."

Herb would always carry a huge wad of cash in his pocket, and he never minded sharing it. He would often take Greg and Dave, along with various other neighborhood kids, to Shea Stadium to watch a baseball game, followed by a meal at a restaurant. And he would always pick up the tab. He was a good-time guy, and everyone liked him.

"If we took vacations, I could always take a friend with me, and he would often take a bunch of us out to the movies," said Dave. "He always had a big bankroll in his pocket, and he was covering everything for everyone. He was a New York guy; he grew up in New York City and was very much cut out of that mold. Then he moved to suburbia but still had that New York edge."

(Young Greg could be generous, too. When he was just a kinder-gartener, he spotted Herb's roll of money lying on an end table in the bedroom and peeled off a hundred-dollar bill, stuffing it in his pocket. When the ice cream man pulled into the neighborhood later that day, Greg handed him the money to buy ice cream for all the kids lined up at the truck and asked, "Is this enough?" Herb didn't even know any money had been taken.)

Herb was also courageous at times. Dave recalls that during one family vacation in Maine, his father spotted a girl struggling in the water offshore, fighting a powerful rip current. "He jumped in the water instantly, swam way out there, and brought her in," he said. "That's the kind of guy he was."

In many ways, Greg felt closer to Herb growing up than he did to his mother and brother. Herb used to take his wife and sons to Florida every summer; he had a lot of family living in the Fort Lauderdale area and kept a second home there. But after a few years, Diane and Dave eventually stopped going. She really didn't like Uncle Donny and the other relatives there. She was smart and opinionated and liked to be in control, but down there she was powerless, and, it was clear, any-thing went.

Herb and Greg started going to Florida alone, driving together in his Cadillac. The Florida house was in a beautiful rural area called Par-adise Village, with corrals, orange groves, and horse farms, and it was certainly a paradise for Greg. He would be gone each day from dawn to nightfall, swimming in the canals—in spite of the alligators—canoe-ing, and catching snakes and giant catfish.

"The house was great," said Greg. "It had orange groves all around it and a canal running right through the backyard. I used to catch cat-fish at night, drag them across the lawn, and put them in the bathtub. They were huge. I'd mess with them all night and let them go in the morning."

One day his father came to the bathroom door, wondering why Greg had been in there so long.

"What are you doing in there, fishing?" he asked.

"Yeah, you wanna see what I got?"

Herb opened the door and peered inside. Swimming around in the bathtub were two giant catfish and an alligator gar—a particularly vicious fish.

"You're crazy!" said Herb, laughing. "But get those fucking things back in the water before they die." He was used to Greg's antics and didn't get mad at him. But he immediately made him carry each of the fish from the bathtub to the canal and release them.

Meanwhile, in Connecticut, Diane was grooming Greg's brother for a different kind of life. From early on, Dave had been a brilliant student and a star athlete, and Diane strongly encouraged his academic pursuits, eventually sending him to a private school. She was a strong, impressive woman but could be overbearing, and Greg always felt like a screw-up in her eyes. Although he was a bright kid, his learning disabilities made it difficult to keep up with his schoolwork. Diane nagged him constantly and pushed him to be more like his brother. So Greg avoided her as much as possible, even as a child, and would spend days at a time camping in their backyard to be by himself. Herb took little part in the raising of their sons and let Diane do whatever she wanted with Dave and Greg's upbringing.

Like a chameleon, Diane was able to fit in with whatever group of people surrounded her. Although she'd been raised Catholic, whenever she was with Greg's Jewish relatives she dressed, behaved, and spoke like a Jewish woman. When she was with mobsters, she acted like a gangster's wife. And when she was with her teaching colleagues, she was just like them: intelligent, well-read, and opinionated.

"People respected her because she was really smart and a great teacher, but she was always pushy, pushy, pushy," said Greg. "And I hated it."

In addition to the mob parties, Herb and Diane would host huge family reunions for the Myerson clan. Herb's aunt, Bess Myerson, was their most famous relative and lived in New York City. A celebrity, she looked the part: always stunning, with immaculate hairdo, makeup, and clothes. Greg remembers how impressive she looked one time she visited: movie star beautiful, with dark glasses and shimmering jewelry, dazzling everyone around her—except Uncle Al, who promptly picked her up, carried her to the edge of the pool, and threw her in with a great splash. She scrambled out and stood up, drenched to the skin, her hairdo ruined and mascara running down her face. "You son of a bitch, Al!" she screamed. But then she started laughing and joined the party. Greg's mother brought her some dry clothes to wear.

It was different with Diane's family when they gathered at his maternal grandmother's house on the holidays. Diane and her two sisters had strong opinions and often held divergent political views. The parties would always turn into screaming matches between them. This was the one time Greg couldn't stand to be at his grandmother's house, and he would often just leave, walking all the way back to his family home, four miles away.

TRAPPER GREG

Everyone in elementary school thought Ron and Matt Bortlein were weird—even the teachers. The brothers, a year apart in age, always kept to themselves and rarely spoke to anyone. Part of the problem was their bullet-headed look. At a time in the mid-1970s when most boys wore their hair longer, the Bortleins' father would take his electric hair clippers every weekend and buzz their hair down to the nubs, giving them an escaped convict look. And their clothes were just not cool: they wore denim dungarees, flannel shirts, and work boots most of the year, and white T-shirts in summer. The boys also had an unusual way of speaking, garbled and unusually deep for children. They would look down when spoken to and seemed unable to engage in conversation. So Ron and Matt walked the mean hallways of their school as pariahs.

"They were always really quiet," said Greg. "They wouldn't talk to anyone, and no one really talked to them, except to harass them." And the Bortlein brothers never fought back when kids picked on them. Mild mannered and self-effacing, they just tried their best not to attract any attention. But Greg noticed them. He's always been drawn to underdogs, and he wanted to know more about them. They were not good students and seemed to have no use for school. They just wanted to get through the day and leave as quickly as possible so they could go out into the woods to hunt and fish. Greg would sometimes run into them there, carrying .22 rifles to hunt rabbits, squirrels, and other small game for their family. They were living a Depression-era life like the television family in *The Waltons*.

Ron and Matt would walk miles each day, deep into the Water Authority forest that surrounded a nearby reservoir. No one but staff was legally allowed inside; it was encircled by chain-link fencing with barbed wire on top and had a padlocked gate to admit Water Authority trucks. When they got to know Greg better, the brothers showed him a secret way to get into the place unseen, but it involved a tough, six-mile hike each way. It was a magical world, where deer were common at a time when they were rarely seen in the other woods Greg frequented. He started hanging around with the Bortleins almost every day, joining them on their long hikes through the woods and becoming very fit. Some days they'd take fly rods and fish for the numerous native brook trout in the streams flowing into the reservoir. Other days they'd hunt small game with their .22 rifles.

Ron and Matt's father had a goose blind in the corn stubble field behind their house, and they invited Greg to come over one day after school to hunt with their father. When Greg stepped off the school bus at the Bortleins' house that afternoon, some of the other boys on the bus heckled him. "You going to hang out with your new best friends, Greggie?" He ignored them.

Later, he and the Bortlein brothers hid in the blind and watched as their father shot two Canada geese. Greg was completely awed and knew this was exactly the way he wanted to live his life. He didn't care what other people thought of him. He admired the skills of the Bortleins and their deep knowledge of woodcraft, and he wanted to learn from them.

"They were good at everything I wanted to do," said Greg. "They were just great outdoorsmen—they lived to hunt and fish and hike through the woods. Everyone made fun of them, but I thought they were cool."

The Bortleins began sharing their world with him. They told Greg they were fur trappers and had a network of traplines running all through the local marshes and riverbanks. That's why they went to the woods every day—to check their traps and harvest any beaver, mink, or muskrats they might have caught. They were as skilled as nineteenth-century trappers, and Greg was eager to learn all about it.

Ron and Matt must have enjoyed having a new friend. They generously taught him everything they knew about trapping: the best places to find muskrats and other animals to catch; what to use for bait; how to set the traps.

For each set, they would pound a metal stake into the mud in the water, a couple of feet from the bank, and attach a length of chain to it with a jawed trap on the other end. They would leave just enough slack in the chain so the trap could sit on the bank, at the very edge of the water. That way, the instant the trap snapped shut on a muskrat's leg, it would fall into the water, and the weight of the trap would drag the animal underwater and drown it. So the animals they caught were almost always dead when they came to get them. But one day, a huge raccoon was caught in one of their traps, and it snarled and lunged toward them as they approached. Ron, the elder of the brothers—always a fierce, no-nonsense hunter and trapper—didn't hesitate. Making a flying dive at the raccoon, he grabbed it with his bare hands and plunged into the river, holding the struggling animal underwater against his chest until it was dead. Ron was scratched, bleeding, and drenched from head to foot when he finally stood up, holding the raccoon limp in his arms. Greg shook his head in amazement. He knew this guy was hardcore.

One day, Greg happened to mention that his grandmother lived on the banks of the Muddy River in North Haven. The two brothers glanced at each other. "That's a great place to trap," said Ron. They offered to sell Greg three traps and help him set them near his grandmother's house. This was on a Sunday, and Greg figured he could wait until the following weekend to check the traps. But that's not how it's done. You need to check traps at least once a day so you can retrieve a trapped animal and prepare its hide as soon as possible after it's caught. The Bortleins got up well before dawn each day to check their traps, and checked them again after school.

Greg's traps hadn't been out a single day when the Bortleins called his house. Greg's mom took the call and told him about it as soon as he got home.

"Who is Matt Bortlein?" she asked as she sat puffing a cigarette at the kitchen table.

"He's just a kid at school," said Greg.

"Oh—he sounded like an old man," said Diane. "Well, he just called and said you have three muskrats in your traps." She stared at him with a look of sheer astonishment as she took another drag on her cigarette. "What the hell is he talking about?"

Greg stared back blankly and shrugged. He walked out to the garage to use the extension phone and called the Bortleins, but no one answered. After a few tries, he jumped on his bike and rode down to the Muddy River, four miles away. Ron and Matt were sitting on the riverbank waiting when he arrived. They hadn't touched the traps, but they wanted Greg to know about the muskrats he had caught. He was amazed that they had come all the way over here to check his traps for him.

"But that was their life," said Greg. "They were always out in the woods and swamps, and knew everything that was going on there."

In addition to teaching Greg how to trap, the Bortleins showed him how to prepare the pelts for market, skinning the muskrat by turning its hide inside out, then stretching it on a rack. The resulting fur pelts were beautiful. They also told him where to sell his pelts and how much money he should receive for them. Trapping was quite a lucrative activity. Muskrats were numerous in the area, and each pelt they sold to a fur buyer in Wallingford could bring ten to twelve dollars or more, depending on its size and condition. Greg was all in. His level of ambition as an eight-year-old was phenomenal.

Although Ron and Matt were shrewd young businessmen, their entrepreneurial instincts were no match for Greg's, and trapping opened up endless possibilities for him. Maybe he would finally be able to earn enough money to buy a small motorboat so he could go fishing anytime he liked in Long Island Sound—an idea that had never left his mind since he first went striped bass fishing with the Carlsons. He quickly became obsessed with trapping and surpassed the Bortleins' efforts. Soon he had dozens of traps set up and down the river and in several other locations.

Scott Jackson, Greg's close friend from special ed class, often joined him in his trapping. Earlier, they had always seemed to be running into each other in the woods, and Greg had wondered how Scott kept finding him. Months later, Scott confessed that one day when he was at Greg's house, he had pulled out his pocketknife and cut a deep notch in one of the lugs of Greg's Vibram-soled boots, giving it a unique tread pattern that showed up well, whether he was hiking in dirt, mud, or snow, so he was able to follow him anywhere easily. Greg had had no idea. They both laughed about it.

Greg and Scott spent a lot of time hanging out at Scott's home, an isolated two-story farmhouse surrounded by plowed fields and farmland. Scott's brother Brian would often torment the two boys. Four years older than them, Brian was powerfully built and athletic, and he could be incredibly brutal. Even though they were just grade-school kids, he would often slap them around and take their money, sometimes leaving them tied up in the basement. They did everything they could to keep out of his way.

"I remember one time we walked into the basement, and he was hiding, hanging from the rafters above the door, waiting for us," said Greg. "When we came in, he dropped down and beat the shit out of us."

A few years later, Brian held his family's home under siege for several days, in a drunken, drugged rage. He locked the house and barred the windows. His parents managed to flee and called the police, who came and surrounded the house. Scott climbed out an upstairs window and was rescued by the fire department with a fire-truck ladder. As a policeman tried to climb up the ladder, Brian threw a toilet seat he'd torn from the bathroom at the policeman, striking him hard and gashing his head. Eventually, the police turned off the water main for the house, waited for him to get thirsty enough to come outside, then jumped him and took him to jail. It wasn't the first—or last—time he would be incarcerated, or that his path would cross with Greg's.

Greg and Scott didn't have a state license to trap, but it seemed pretty safe—no one else was trapping on the stretch of the Muddy River near his grandmother's house. But as Greg started branching out to other places, he soon got into trouble. He started trapping in some prime areas where special permits chosen by lottery were required. It didn't take long for one of the other trappers to stumble upon some of his traps. When Greg came to check them, he found that several had been smashed with a hammer and ruined. He didn't care; he just set new traps in their place, and tried to make them less visible. But then things took a serious turn.

One night Greg was collecting the muskrats he'd caught and resetting his traps in one of the best areas. He was using a flashlight so he could see what he was doing, which made him visible from a long distance. Suddenly, *bang!*—a gunshot echoed across the river and a bullet came screaming past, only a foot or two above him. Greg instantly hit the ground, dropping his flashlight into the water. He lay there in the darkness, shivering in terror, his face pressed hard into the mud. A second later, *bang! bang!*—two more bullets ripped past. For a long time, he didn't dare move, but he could hear the *blub-blub-blub-blub* of a small outboard motor idling out there somewhere, perhaps a couple hundred yards away. After a while, the sound faded, then vanished entirely. Greg was sure it was the other trapper, the one who'd destroyed his traps, trying to scare him off. And he *was* scared, at first—but then he could feel his face start to burn with anger. He had to get back at this guy somehow.

Greg talked to Scott about it later that night, and they planned their revenge. Each of them had a .22 rifle, and they decided to bring them along the next time they went to check their traps. They pulled together all the ammunition they had and put the bullets into ten-round clips that they could easily switch whenever they emptied their guns.

The next night they went back to the place where Greg had been shot at, but this time they set up a bright lantern there, then hiked fifty yards away into the darkness and crouched in the reeds, where they waited . . . and waited . . . and waited. It was nearly midnight when Greg finally heard the familiar *blub-blub-blub-blub* of the outboard motor. He knew it was the same guy, but they waited to see what he was going to do. *Bang!* A shot pierced the stillness.

That was all it took. Greg and Scott unleashed a massive fusillade, firing their rifles wildly in the general direction the shot came from, filling the air with bullets and gun smoke. They had no idea if their bullets were going anywhere near the man, and they didn't care. If he got hit, so be it. In their minds, he had it coming. Each of them fired more than a hundred rounds, switching clips and reloading again and again and again until they were out of ammo. And then they just lay back and laughed till their stomachs hurt, imagining the terrified man hunkered down flat in the bottom of his dinghy, cringing fearfully as the bullets tore past in the darkness, hoping and praying he wouldn't be hit. No one ever bothered them there again.

Greg was determined to earn as much money as possible, so he also worked on a vegetable farm between fur-trapping seasons. (The quality of the furs is poor during the warm-weather months of spring and summer, and fur trapping is legal in Connecticut from early November to early March.) The farm's owner, Charlie Valentino, had come to make a payment on a gambling debt, and Greg and Scott were hanging around the backyard as Valentino spoke with Herb.

"Why don't you hire these fucking assholes so I don't have to put up with their bullshit anymore?" said Herb, nodding toward Greg and Scott. Valentino did. Later that day, the boys walked down to the farm and began picking tomatoes in his field.

Valentino was a middle-aged Italian immigrant, and he always wore white painter's overalls as he worked side by side with them in the fields. After that meeting with Herb, he addressed the boys the way Herb had: "Hey, why don't you fucking assholes help me pick the zucchini?"

Once, when they were all picking tomatoes, Scott threw one at Greg, hitting him in the back of the head with a loud *splat!* Greg whirled around, but Scott nodded toward Charlie Valentino. Greg grabbed a tomato and hurled it at the man as he bent over the tomatoes, splattering the back of his white overalls with red juice. Valentino was furious, but he didn't fire Greg, perhaps fearing Herb's wrath. He glared at Greg and Scott, his face burning red with anger, but just turned back to his work.

A BIG FISH

At first, most of Greg's trapping activities took place without the knowledge of his parents. But one day he was boiling traps in a big aluminum pot full of water and beeswax (to waterproof them) on a log fire in the woods behind his house, when his father came out to see what he was doing. "What the hell is this?" he said. "It looks like a goddamn hobo camp."

Greg shrugged and tried to avoid talking about it. Herb let it go at first. He had no idea what his son was up to. It wasn't until months later that his parents began to realize the scope of what he was doing.

One day Greg asked his mother if she would drive him to Wallingford so he could sell his muskrat pelts to a fur dealer, and after some hesitation she agreed. At this point he'd been trapping for almost two years and had nearly 600 pelts stored neatly in a chest freezer in the garage.

"I had them stacked really thin, arranged from extra-large to large, medium, and small," said Greg. "The Bortleins taught me all that. When I got to the fur dealer, I had everything laid out. I pretty much knew the prices, so the guy really couldn't cheat me."

Diane was astounded as Greg pulled out box after box of beautifully prepared hides, each one sorted by size and quality. But that didn't prepare her for the shock when the fur dealer gave Greg a check for more than $5,000, which he deposited into his own bank account. He was ten years old.

Greg now had enough money to buy a boat, so he got his Aunt Cookie to drive him to Richard Brockway's home in Old Saybrook, Connecticut. Brockway was renowned for the wooden skiffs he built in his backyard, and Greg wanted one badly. He gave Brockway a down payment of $2,000 so he would start building his boat.

What Greg was doing did not sit well with Herb. Not that he objected to the initiative Greg showed in earning the money to buy his own boat—he thought that was great. It was the way he was doing it. Call him a mobster with a heart of gold, but Herb had always loved animals and had given generously to the Humane Society. He proudly displayed a trophy on his mantel presented to him by the organization in appreciation of his many contributions over the years. (He had also given substantial financial support to Native American causes.) Herb begged Greg to stop trapping.

"I can't let this happen, Greg," he said. "This is brutal." But Greg was adamant that he would keep on trapping.

"Look, if you stop trapping animals, I will pay for the rest of the goddamn boat," said Herb. "Please. Just stop."

Greg didn't say anything, but he knew there was nothing his father could say that would stop him from doing what he wanted. He had enough money to pay for the boat anyway. He just needed to earn a little more to buy a motor.

A short time later, just before Christmas, Herb went to see Mr. Brockway and paid him cash for the balance Greg owed. He had the boat delivered to the house and put it in the garage. It was sitting there on Christmas morning as a present for Greg.

"My dad thought I would just stop trapping, because I already had the boat," said Greg. "But there was no way that was going to happen. That was how I made my money."

When Herb finally put his foot down and said he had to get rid of his traps, Greg just nodded and left the room. He packed up all of his trapping equipment and took it to his grandmother's house, and that became the center of his trapping business. He started spending more and more time there, sleeping there every weekend and living there all summer long. He had his own room. No one would ever be able to set rules for him again.

Greg bought an old Evinrude outboard motor for his skiff and started fishing almost every day—at first with Aunt Cookie. She helped him get a slip at the Branford docks.

"We went there three or four times a week," said Aunt Cookie. "We started at maybe twelve or one in the afternoon and didn't leave until dark. That's how much Greg loved fishing." He was so competent, she felt like she never had to worry about him. He was very athletic even at that age and knew exactly how to run the motor and maneuver the boat in any situation. "He could back up that Brockway as good as you could park a car," she said.

Greg loved Aunt Cookie, but it was a mixed blessing having her with him when he went fishing. Although she was always eager and enthusiastic, she wouldn't let him take the boat out of the harbor. The only time he talked her into going into Long Island Sound, she got seasick, so that was that.

Sometimes Greg fished with a friend from elementary school, but more often he went by himself. He loved the solitude of being alone with nature, with no one to answer to and no one that he had to please. He could escape the turmoil of his home life and do whatever he wanted. Each day after school, he would ride his bike ten miles to the harbor where his boat was tied up and take it out. His parents insisted that he stay inside Branford Harbor, and he assured them he would—but he broke that rule every time he went fishing, sometimes cruising for miles up and down the coast to search for fish. He fished in all kinds of weather, without any navigational equipment or a two-way radio. This is when his relationship with the striped bass truly began.

Greg started thinking again about the Race, where he'd first gone striper fishing with the Carlsons a couple of years earlier, and he longed to go back there by himself. It was a crazy idea. Mr. Carlson had a well-equipped sport-fishing boat more than thirty feet long, with a two-way radio and full electronic navigational equipment. Greg had none of that, just a small open boat with an old Evinrude motor, yet he planned to take it to one of the most treacherous stretches of water in the area, where Long Island Sound meets the open Atlantic Ocean. When the tide is changing, rushing in or out, a colossal amount of water gets pinched through a skinny space, less than four miles wide, creating a surging maelstrom of boat-rocking water and a powerful rip. Over the centuries, countless crafts, both large and small, have gone down there, with a huge loss of life. According to local legend, the old lighthouse on Race Rock—at the entrance to the Race—is haunted by the ghosts of seamen who perished there. (The lighthouse was once featured on the popular television show *Ghost Hunters*.)

Greg set out alone one morning from Branford Harbor, heading eastward to the Race, nearly twenty miles away. With his tiny motor chugging along, it would take nearly four hours to get there on a good day. But about three hours into his journey, a fog bank rolled in, blanketing the area for miles around and cutting his visibility to less than ten feet. He was functionally blind, with no electronics to guide him, no radio, not even a compass. He had no way to see where he was going, what rocks he might be approaching, or whether a boat or ship might be cruising toward him.

"I couldn't see anything," said Greg. "Boats were going by me, almost running me over."

But then he heard the distant moan of the foghorn at Race Rock lighthouse and headed his boat toward the sound.

As he reached the lighthouse, a sport-fishing boat loomed suddenly through the fog. It was anchored just off Race Rock, with the skipper waiting for the fog to lift. He shouted at Greg when his little boat emerged from the fog. "What the hell are you doing here, kid? You're going to get killed." He was older, perhaps in his sixties, with a grizzled face and red-rimmed eyes. He tied Greg's skiff to the stern of his boat, and the two of them fished together.

An hour later, Greg felt a tug on the end of his line and jerked the rod tip upward to set the hook in the fish's mouth. The fish tugged back, and it was like nothing he'd ever felt before—the sheer brute power of this fish as it peeled line off his reel. He knew instantly it was much bigger than any fish he'd caught with the Carlsons, and he fought it with all his might, trying to turn it as it swam hard away from him. After nearly an hour, Greg was breathing hard, but he finally had the fish alongside, and it was enormous—the biggest striped bass he had ever seen. The man had a large landing net and swung it up under the fish, but even with the two of them, it was hard to get the fish into the boat. When they weighed it, it topped out at just over fifty pounds. Greg had caught his first huge striped bass, but it had also caught him.

As soon as he got back to the harbor, he put the bass in his red wagon and pulled it around town to show the fish off to everyone he knew. His family never suspected how far he had gone to catch the huge bass; none of them knew anything about fishing.

"I told everyone I caught it in Branford Harbor," said Greg. "It was huge. My family ate it, and it was just the greatest thing."

Unfortunately, several sport-fishing party boats had seen Greg out there that day and several other times and had been complaining to the Coast Guard about this fool kid in a little boat who was going way out to sea and was going to get himself killed. Nothing happened at first, but the Coast Guard had Greg on its radar and was making every effort to catch him. One day they finally succeeded.

"The Coast Guard tied my boat up to theirs and towed it in to port," said Greg. "Then they called my parents. They had to drive all the way to Old Lyme to get me. I was in a shitload of trouble, but I was so unruly, I didn't even care. They told me I couldn't use the boat anymore, but I used it anyway." Greg was ten years old and already completely incorrigible.

GRIDIRON GLORY

In junior high, Greg was often picked on not only by bullies but also by some of the teachers and coaching staff, who were furious that Dave, the star athlete, had left to attend a prestigious private school called Hamden Hall and was now tearing it up on the baseball field and gridiron there. They seemed determined to take their frustrations out on Greg. To understand their position you need to know how important athletics—and especially baseball—were to the junior and senior high schools in North Haven, and how the coaches had envisioned Dave Myerson's vital role in the time they thought he would be there. Even in junior high, Dave was a fabulous baseball player.

"He was the greatest pitcher they'd ever seen there," said Greg. "He averaged eight strikeouts a game all through growing up."

Dozens of people would come to baseball games at the school and in the Babe Ruth League just to see Dave pitch—he was that good. Everyone knew he was going places, and they wanted to be able to say they'd seen him play when he was young. When the North Haven coaches imagined the next three or four high school baseball seasons, with Dave as their star pitcher, they saw state championships and endless glory for the schools—and for themselves. That all vanished in an instant when he switched schools. Losing Dave staggered them.

The faculty and coaches no doubt reasoned, *Why should we do anything to help Greg's athletic career? If he ever amounts to anything as a baseball or football player, he'll probably just transfer away like his brother.* It was a shortsighted, petty, and small-minded attitude, and one certainly unbefitting public educators. Besides, they were only shooting themselves in the foot. Greg had no desire to attend Hamden Hall. Diane would have gladly sent him there but he didn't want any part of it. That was Dave's thing; it wasn't for him. Greg had always had such a hard time with his schoolwork, because of his dyslexia, he no doubt shuddered at the thought of attending such a highbrow school.

Despite the lack of support, Greg tried hard to succeed in his junior high school in North Haven. He joined the football team in seventh and eighth grades and could have made a great contribution if only the coaches had chosen to make use of his great athletic potential. But he got no respect there. In two entire football seasons, they let him play only once—in the final minute of a single game. That was it: his entire junior high school football career. So he became disgusted with the whole thing and lost interest in team sports.

Fortunately, when he was thirteen, Greg found out about a vocational agriculture program in natural resources at Lyman Hall High School, and he jumped at the chance to escape from North Haven. Lyman Hall was full of working-class kids with low expectations, about as far removed as you could get from a private school. But Greg knew that transferring there would give him a chance to reinvent himself. He had no interest in becoming an athlete or doing any other extracurricular activities. He just wanted to be left alone to do what he loved most—go fishing. But he was already growing toward his adult size when the school year began, and he quickly caught the attention of Lyman Hall's coaching staff. They had no qualms about taking advantage of Greg's talents. Head football coach Phil Ottochian spotted Greg walking in the hallway on the first day of school and stopped him.

"Hey, you're going to play football," he told him. "Be at the practice field right after school today."

Greg had no athletic clothes or equipment and had to wear his blue jeans and boots and scrounge up some pads and a helmet in the locker room for that first practice. But he was good, and the coaching staff instantly saw his potential. In his very first game as a freshman, Lyman Hall hammered the Branford High School team—and Greg was the star, sacking the quarterback, slamming hard into running backs, and physically throwing people out of bounds, at times being far more violent and aggressive than necessary to make a play. It was as if a tiger locked inside him had been unleashed.

Greg was an instant success on the football field, accepted and embraced by everyone at Lyman Hall, and he became captain of the freshman team that first season. He was so strong and determined—a born leader who inspired everyone around him. But something had changed in him. Perhaps it was partly the frustration he felt because of his father's illness. Two years earlier, Herb had been diagnosed with Parkinson's disease. At first his symptoms were barely noticeable, but by the time Greg started at Lyman Hall, Herb's physical condition had begun to deteriorate significantly. Or perhaps it was his mother's constant efforts to micromanage his life. Or maybe he had just been picked on and pushed around for such a long time it made some kind of explosion inevitable. A kind of brutality overtook him.

"I just wanted to kill everyone," said Greg. "Before I started playing football, I had no idea how much aggression I had pent up inside me. I had been this quiet kid who always got beat up. But I was getting pretty big and really athletic."

It's not that he had become a bully: he was actually the exact opposite. He knew what it was like to be bullied, and he became the protector of many students who were being picked on—people like his old trapping buddy Ron Bortlein, who entered the vo-ag program at the same time as Greg and rode with him to Lyman Hall every day on a school shuttle bus. He never let anyone hassle Ron, and he convinced other people that Ron was a good guy and worth knowing.

"Other kids started talking to Ron and treating him like a friend," said Greg. "I think it was a very happy time in his life."

But Greg could be brutal to anyone who made him mad. "I started to become a real tough guy," he said. "I wouldn't take any crap from anyone at that point. My father was sick, and I was pissed off at the world." In high school, he often had black eyes and scratches like he'd just been in a brawl.

Greg became close friends with Vinny Poggio, one of the best football players on the Lyman Hall team. Perhaps the fact that they both were dealing with tough situations at home drew them closer. Less than a year earlier, a devastating tragedy had struck Vinny's family during a hundred-year flood that swept through the area. Vinny and his two older brothers, Richie (fifteen years old) and Bobby (sixteen), had taken a wild ride in a small inflatable raft down Wharton Brook, a stream behind their house that was usually tiny but had become a raging torrent in the flood. Their raft hit a half-submerged tree and got sucked under and ripped. The three of them smashed hard into the tree trunk. Vinny and Bobby were able to swim to the side of the swollen brook and drag themselves out of the water on all fours, but they didn't see Richie. Could he have been knocked out by the tree? Or had he dragged himself out somewhere downstream? They began searching frantically in the driving rain and calling his name, but it was useless; they could barely see or hear anything. Vinny ran to their house, which was right beside the stream, and called 911 while Bobby kept looking.

Everyone went searching for Richie—the Civil Air Patrol (which led the effort all through the following day), other kids from his high school, and people throughout the community. But the newspapers were already saying that Richie had been "swept away and was believed drowned." And he wasn't the only one: at least six other people in that part of Connecticut were missing and presumed dead after the flood, and several other bodies had already been recovered. It was an epic flood, breaching dams, washing away bridges, and knocking out power for hundreds of thousands of people.

As two days passed, most of the searchers had stopped looking—except for Richie's father, whose voice was still heard calling, "Richie! Richie!" three nights later from the woods up and down the brook. On the fourth day, after the flood had receded, one of Richie's friends from school found him, half buried in sand far downstream from where he had vanished. Richie had been a high school sophomore, only a year older than Vinny. He and his family were devastated.

This had happened in early June, and the varsity team at Lyman Hall invited Vinny to practice with them for the entire summer, hoping it might help keep his mind occupied as he tried to deal with this overwhelming tragedy.

Greg met Vinny on his first day of school at Lyman Hall, and they became friends immediately. They played together on the football team, Vinny running many of the touchdowns (no one could catch him) and Greg making spectacular tackles. They both made All-State and All-American. Vinny was an amazing tailback and still holds all the running records at Lyman Hall. But they were also close friends away from the field (and still are to this day; Greg lives right next door to Vinny's elderly mother).

Greg bears a striking resemblance to Vinny's dead brother Richie. Although he never met him, Greg has seen many pictures of him and their similarity is uncanny. Perhaps at some level, Vinny and his family realized that. His parents embraced Greg like another son, making him one of their own. He would live at their house for weeks at a time, and it had a soothing effect on him. It felt so comfortable to stay there with them, with none of the stresses he faced at home.

"It was weird how they completely accepted me into their family," said Greg. "It was like I was one of them. They loved me and would do anything for me."

With his long blond hair, which always hung out of the bottom of his football helmet, Vinny looked like a California beach kid. He was also an excellent skateboarder. Perhaps as a way to deal with his grief, Vinny smoked pot constantly, and Greg started smoking it with him. They were always skateboarding and getting high together. Greg was also drinking heavily, something he had already been doing before he met Vinny. Herb still had connections with the liquor business, so there was always plenty of alcohol around the house. But it was Vinny's brother Bob who first introduced Greg to cocaine, when he was fifteen years old, and to a large extent it soon took over his life.

"When I snorted coke, it was like everything disappeared—my father's illness, all the bullshit going on in my life, it just didn't matter anymore," said Greg. "But no one knew I was doing it. I was a good kid. I did my schoolwork. I was an athlete. Fishing all the time. But I was using all that shit. I got into it young and stuck with it. At the time, I saw it almost as a medicine, something to make me feel better. I never did anything horrible to get it, but I wish I'd never started taking it."

Greg lived in a tough town, and many of his friends ended up abusing drugs and alcohol or getting into trouble with the police. One boy on his football team would often show up late—and drunk—as the bus was waiting to take them to a game. He'd get on the bus and be crying. Everyone would get out of his way and he'd sit down, reeking of booze. No one said anything. Amazingly, he was one of the best players on the team.

"He had college scholarship offers everywhere to go play football, but he was just too messed up to do it," said Greg.

Herb's view of Greg changed drastically one day at the end of one of his football games. They were walking out to the parking lot after watching a game that Greg's team had lost. Herb and Diane were following about twenty feet behind him. Greg overheard a woman behind him say that he was a dirty player, and he turned and shouted into her face, "Fuck you, lady!"

"Gregory!" his mother cried out, appalled.

A football player from another high school who had come to watch the game said to Greg, "Better watch your mouth!"

Greg snapped, kicking him hard in the balls, then beating him senseless while other people tried to pull him away.

After that, Herb looked at him differently, perhaps recognizing his own ferocity in Greg. Herb's illness was worsening, making his job as a bookmaker much more difficult. One day soon after that game, he asked Greg if he wanted to make some money, and Greg became a bagman for Herb, picking up cash and delivering it to him, for which Herb would pay him a couple hundred dollars.

"I had my car, my grandmother's 1970 Chevy Nova that she gave me," said Greg. "I was sixteen and doing the collecting—and smoking weed."

Herb told him never under any circumstances to look inside the bag. But the temptation overcame Greg when he was smoking a joint with Scott Jackson, and they unzipped the bag, revealing $30,000 in cash.

"We were like, 'Let's get the hell out of here,'" said Greg. "We decided we were going to steal the money from the mob and drive all the way down to Florida. I don't know what the hell we were thinking. I guess we thought we could just live in Florida forever."

Greg and Scott often pushed against boundaries together. Sometimes they would deliberately go blasting past police speed traps on their motorcycles, going nearly ninety miles per hour, so the cops would chase them. They'd manage to ditch them, going off-road on muddy dirt trails where the squad cars couldn't follow. So they had no qualms about breaking rules.

The two had recently returned from an earlier trip to Florida, where they'd stayed with Greg's Uncle Donny, and it had been a nonstop party. He let them drive his Ferrari around, and they could drink as much as they wanted. "He would buy us beer and shoot his handgun in the streets of Miami at night when he went on walks with us," said Greg. "We'd come to these alleyways and empty lots, and he would let us shoot his pistol. He didn't give a fuck."

He also let them take his speedboat to the Everglades whenever they wanted.

"We would haul ass in that speedboat doing a hundred," said Greg. "We didn't give a shit, and Uncle Donny didn't either. He was cool like that. We loved it."

They hadn't looked up Uncle Donny yet on this trip, but instead had gone straight to Herb's vacation house in Fort Lauderdale. A couple days later they were sitting on the front porch, smoking a big joint, when Herb pulled up in a rental car. He had just flown down from New York. He stepped out of the car, slammed its door, and walked onto the porch. Grabbing the joint from Greg, he took a big hit from it, then tossed it out in the yard.

"Tell me you still have the money," he said, staring grimly at Greg.

"Yeah, we didn't spend any of it," said Greg. "It's all still in the bag."

"Good," he said. "Then there's no harm done." And that was all he said on the matter. But the look in his eyes as he stared at Greg told a different story. This was it, the only reprieve he would ever get. If he ever did anything like this again, he would not be protected by the bonds of blood and would face the full wrath of the mob.

EL CID

In 1985, in Greg's senior year at Lyman Hall High School, his varsity football team miraculously found itself vying for the state high school championship. This was the last team in Connecticut anyone expected to become a contender for this honor. They'd never come close to winning a championship in their entire history. The team didn't even have enough players to break into two teams to practice against each other without having to find non–team members to suit up and play with them.

"Our 'coaching staff' consisted of former players and their friends," said head coach Phil Ottochian. "They dressed up and scrimmaged with our kids. They did a great job."

The year before, the team had been like the Bad News Bears, winning only one or two games the entire season, and they were competing in the toughest league in Connecticut. Everyone said the team would go nowhere.

"We were below underdog—below the surface," said Steve Hoag, the defensive coach at Lyman Hall. But they did have Greg. "He was El Cid," said Hoag, referring to the medieval Spanish leader depicted in the 1961 Charlton Heston film *El Cid*, whose body was mounted on horseback and led a victorious charge against his enemies—even though he was dead.

Greg's toughness and his stoicism in the face of excruciating pain were already legendary. One day in practice, Greg was hit hard, splitting his chin open like a ripe cantaloupe. He went to the locker room and tried to patch it up with large Band-Aids, but he was bleeding all over the place, so he went home, took a needle and fishing line, and stitched up his face. "Fourteen or fifteen stitches," said Hoag. "He looked like a rag doll. No drama, no nothing. That was Greg."

Greg played many positions for the Lyman Hall Trojans. He had to, since there were so few players. During the course of the season he was the team's kicker, a defensive end, a guard, and the center. When a fullback got hurt, Greg played fullback for a few games. He excelled at everything he tried.

The Lyman Hall Trojans were one game away from making it to the state championship and had to play against their cross-town rival, Sheehan High School. They absolutely had to beat them, after which they'd face the reigning state champions, Middletown High School, a nationally ranked team. Hoag and head coach Phil Ottochian had gone to Sheehan High School to scout, when a sportswriter from a local newspaper approached them.

"You know, it'd probably be better if you lose on Thanksgiving, so you won't have to face Middletown," he said, laughing. "Do you have any idea how good they are?" Everyone knew the team's reputation: Middletown had won twenty-two straight games, averaging forty-four points a game. The players had no concept of defeat. They hadn't even been behind in a game for a couple of seasons.

The Lyman Hall game against Sheehan was postponed for one day, after a massive snowstorm struck on Thanksgiving. To the surprise of everyone, the Lyman Hall Trojans absolutely slaughtered the Sheehan Titans, playing in brutally tough weather conditions on a snowy field and beating them 40–0. So the stage was set for an epic showdown: the Middletown Blue Dragons against the upstart Lyman Hall Trojans.

The championship game was played at Memorial Stadium at the University of Connecticut, and it was packed—more than 14,000 spectators had come to see the high school football game, including the entire student body of UConn and numerous coaches from top colleges looking for new recruits. The Blue Dragons were a sight to behold as they strode onto the field, looking more like NFL players than high school athletes. (Nine of their eleven starters went on to play Division I football in college.) Even their uniforms were as impressive as any worn by pros. Their band began playing the instant the team stepped onto the field, and their fans cheered. But Greg was unimpressed and taunted them mercilessly before the game as his teammates were doing their stretches.

"They'd run by me, and I'd say, 'You're dead! You're done! This is fucking it for you, man!'" said Greg. "They'd look at me like I was crazy, knowing how good they were."

Lyman Hall had the kickoff. Although Greg kicked the ball deep down the field, Middletown ran it all the way back through the Lyman Hall defense, a spectacular eighty-eight-yard return, scoring a convincing touchdown in the opening seconds of the game. A collective groan —mixed with laughter from the Middletown fans—went up from the crowd.

"They came down and were everything they were supposed to be," said Coach Hoag. "They nailed our guys. It was like, okay, as advertised, let's go. Like a beautiful woman, here's what it is." Right after the play, he overheard someone in the press box offering forty-to-one odds against Lyman Hall.

So the Trojans had their backs against the wall right from the beginning. The Middletown Blue Dragons had more than sixty players, with separate offense and defense. Greg's team, by contrast, had only eight good players, and the rest just filled out the empty spots. Everyone had to play both offense and defense. But this made the Lyman Hall team much tougher.

"We were a really well-oiled team, in great physical shape, because we went through the whole season going both ways," said Greg. "Everyone on the team was in the peak physical condition of their life at that point."

The Middletown fans roared as their defensive team took to the field, overflowing with confidence, ready to put the final nail in Lyman Hall's coffin. Greg and his teammates knew they had to calm down and start playing their game if they were to have any chance of stopping these guys.

"Vinny took the first handoff," said Greg. "We blew them right off the line, and he was gone for a touchdown. Then we went for two points, threw a pass, and suddenly we were ahead."

So they were instantly back in the game. Greg kicked off again, and this time they held them. Lyman Hall got the ball back and scored again, and they just kept scoring, intercepting Middletown's passes, sacking the quarterback, moving the ball forward aggressively, making first downs and scoring touchdowns. By the end of the first quarter, the score stood at 22–6—the first time in more than two years that the Middletown Blue Dragons had been behind in a game.

Middletown tried everything that first half, to no avail—but it was clear that the Blue Dragons could come roaring back at any second, scoring at will. That's certainly what most people watching the game that day expected. And then the nightmare scenario happened: with four minutes left till halftime, Greg went down hard—and he didn't get up.

"We had rules that we weren't supposed to run out on the field when a player was down; we would only let the trainer go," said Coach Hoag. "But as soon as I saw Greg lying there, I ran out to him. He'd always seemed so indestructible. He had a threshold for pain beyond anything I've ever seen. But he was on the ground, and I knew it was bad."

Greg had a separated shoulder, an extremely painful injury. "I was blocking on offense when it happened," said Greg. "I fell in a pile and somehow my shoulder just popped out of the socket. It had been giving me problems the game before that, but then it went. I was lying on the field, and it was excruciating."

An ambulance came onto the field and drove right up to Greg. The attendants took a stretcher out and tried to lift Greg onto it, but he pulled away. "Forget it, I'm not getting into that," he said. As he stood up, his shoulder popped back into place, though the pain was still nearly unbearable. The ambulance attendants tried to persuade him to let them help him but finally gave up, put the stretcher back in the ambulance, and drove back off the field.

The Middletown players were all yelling, "Yeah, we got him! We kicked his ass!"—which made Greg furious. "You guys are all fucking dead now!" he shouted at them.

Dave Myerson and all of his Yale friends had come to the game to support Greg and were in the stands, dressed in raccoon coats and drunk. Dave jumped onto the field, reeking of booze, and walked up to Greg.

"What's the deal, man?" he said. "Are you going to make it or what?"

"Yeah, I'm all right."

"Good! Don't be a pussy," he said.

There was no way Greg would be leaving the game.

"I was watching as my backup was getting exploited to the max—a young kid," Greg told me. "They were running over him. I was saying, put my shit back on."

"We were holding on at the end of the half," said Coach Ottochian. "We were exhausted. We'd taken Greg out of the game and gone with a substitute. We had possession of the ball on the three-yard line, and we didn't score."

The team managed to finish the half without giving up any points, but what would they do in the second half? The only kid they had to sub for Greg was a freshman who had never played in a game.

No one was talking as they walked back to the locker room, but the body language was clearly *Oh, no!* Coach Hoag was near tears as he watched Greg being worked on by a University of Connecticut doctor.

"You know, you spend most halftimes making adjustments to your team," said Hoag. "The only adjustment for us then was, 'Now what?'" They could hear the team in the other locker room whooping it up, psyching themselves up for the next half, knowing that the advantage in the game had shifted strongly toward them.

Greg lay on the table with his jersey and his shoulder pads off, but as the end of the halftime neared, he sat up. "Give me my pads," he said.

"Oh no, son," said the doctor. "You're not going anywhere. Your day is over."

Greg stood up and grabbed his shoulder pads, and a teammate helped him put them on and pull his jersey over his head, his injured arm wrapped in place under his jersey. "I'm playing the second half," he said.

"Sorry, your day is over," repeated the doctor. Greg ignored him and started walking out of the locker room with his teammates, followed closely by the doctor. "Look, you're done, kid. You can't play anymore today."

Greg finally whirled around, grabbed the doctor by the shirt and shoved him hard against the wall. "Look, if I don't play the second half, I will kill you!" he said.

"You could see the doctor's eyes saying, 'I don't think he's kidding,'" said Hoag.

So Greg walked onto the field with his left arm bound to his chest under his jersey and one sleeve blowing in the wind—and Greg is left-handed. "He was playing defensive end, and his left shoulder was hurt, right?" said Coach Ottochian. "So he was playing right-handed with one hand."

The Blue Dragons rallied, throwing everything they had against Lyman Hall, determined to turn the game around, and their effort was paying off. Early in the fourth quarter, Middletown was down by only four points, and they had possession on the Lyman Hall ten-yard line. A single touchdown would put them in the lead. Middletown quarterback Dennis Wade seemed unstoppable, methodically moving the ball forward, pass after pass, while the Trojans ran around all over the place, trying to halt their advance. A sense of despair began moving through the Lyman Hall team. "He's really good," one player said in the huddle. "He's doing whatever he wants with us now," said another. "How can we ever stop him?"

Greg frowned. "Fuck that guy!" he shouted, in a rage. "Let's go fucking kill him!" The intensity of his anger and determination were contagious.

"Yeah, fuck him!" said the others. "Fuck him!" And they stormed back to the line of scrimmage, eager for play to resume.

The instant the center snapped the ball, the Trojans rushed, breaking through the Middletown line and charging toward the quarterback. Two linebackers hit Wade simultaneously, one high and one low, and he folded like an accordion, losing the ball, which went flying straight up nearly twenty feet in the air. Lyman Hall defensive end Ralph Riley leapt up and caught the ball, then ran and ran and ran—all the way to the Middletown goal line, scoring a touchdown and boosting the score to 28–18. The Lyman Hall fans erupted, jumping to their feet and cheering as the Middletown fans sat silently, mouths agape in disbelief.

The Blue Dragons refused to be rattled and came on again more determined than ever. The next time Lyman Hall had possession of the ball, the Middletown team turned their full attention to Greg. Like sharks smelling blood, they sensed he was a weak link they could pry open and come flooding in, sacking the quarterback.

"As hurt as I was, they kept trying to run around my side, but I just kept running them down," said Greg. "They were just like, 'What the fuck!' They had never been behind their whole year. They were really good."

Greg continued to hold firm—"with one arm—*one arm!*" said Coach Hoag, his eyes misting up. "And he played better than anyone.

He was making plays you wouldn't believe. And when I say he was El Cid, it was literally, he got back up on the horse even though he was half dead."

"He was tackling people, rushing and passing, and they still couldn't get to the outside of him," said Ottochian. "That's how good he was. I've always said that I've coached some great players through the years, but Greg was the most talented."

Everyone on the Lyman Hall team rallied, saying, "We're not going to lose this game, no matter what!" By then, the thin crust of snow and ice that had covered the field at the start of the game had melted, creating a muddy bog. As the teams struggled desperately in the mud, throwing themselves at each other again and again, no one willing to give up an inch, the game began to look like the Battle of Agincourt in Kenneth Branagh's film version of Shakespeare's *Henry V*.

At the end of the game, the score still stood at 28–18, with the Lyman Hall Trojans the unlikely victors. And as the players walked off the field, many on both teams limping and bloodied, with torn uniforms, they knew something remarkable had taken place on the field that day.

"There was nothing left," said Greg. "They left it all on the field that day. I've never seen that in any sport. Ever. It was just unbelievable."

Everyone was covered with mud as they walked to the locker room, too dazed to celebrate. Greg remembers seeing Matt Schmitt, a Lyman Hall running back who had run for 100 yards in the game, lying facedown on the shower-room floor, still wearing his helmet and uniform as the water washed over him, mud streaming down the drain.

"He didn't have an ounce of energy left in him," said Greg. "I was the same way. And my arm was killing me. I remember there were ten reporters interviewing me after the game. I had so many microphones in my face; I don't even remember what they asked me. My brother was trying to get in to see me, but he couldn't even get close. He was looking at me and smiling like, 'Have your fucking moment.' I got on the bus later wearing my suit and jacket and tie, and I had my arm in a sling. The town cop, who was about to retire, sat down next to me on the bus, and he pulled out a bottle of whiskey and handed it to me. 'You done good, kid,' he said."

"Even now, more than thirty years later, when any of us from that season get together, Greg is always in the first line of the conversation," said Hoag. "'Do you remember . . . ?' 'Did you hear . . . ?' I run into people who played against us in that state championship game, and they still talk about what he did. He was legendary. He was El Cid. No one who was there that day will ever forget him."

MOB JUSTICE

Near the end of high school, Greg started placing football bets with a small-time local bookie named Marco, who owned a meat market. Greg had seen him a few times at his father's parties and approached him about making some bets. None of the other local bookies would take bets from Greg, because they were afraid of his father, but Marco had some serious gambling debts of his own and needed to make money fast. He owed Herb $30,000 and had been trying to delay paying him.

Greg's betting was a disaster, and he soon owed Marco more than $2,000. Somehow the story got back to Herb, and he was furious about it—but he became absolutely apoplectic when he heard that Marco had tried to make a large bet with another bookie when he still owed money to Herb. The bookie refused his bet and tipped off Herb, who sent Al and Sal and two other goons to pay a visit to Marco at his meat market. He told them to take Greg along to stand guard—and to give him a glimpse of the perils of the gambling life.

Greg climbed into the back seat of the red Cadillac Eldorado and rode to the meat market with the four men. As they started walking to the door, Al turned and said, "Hey Greg, go back and get the duct tape. I left it on the floor by the front seat." Greg grabbed the tape and caught up with the men as they were entering the shop. Marco blanched when he saw them. He was standing at the cash register, taking care of an elderly woman buying some pork chops.

"Hey, we're closed now," said Sal as he ushered the woman outside. He flipped the sign in the window around to read "Closed" and turned to Marco. "You know, you really should pay your bills on time," he said, glaring at him. Marco trembled.

Sal told Greg to watch the door and tell anyone who tried to enter that the shop was closed. Al cleaned out all the money in the cash register—more than $800. The other two men went behind the counter and grabbed Marco by the arms.

"What are you going to do?" he asked, frantically. No one answered. Sal unbuckled the man's belt and pulled down his pants and boxer shorts. "Oh, God, please . . . don't do this. I can get you the money soon, I swear."

"Bend over and grab your ankles," said Sal.

"You know you can take anything you want from here . . . hams, steaks . . . anything," said Marco. Al, who was standing nearby, smiled and pulled a big, long salami from the meat cabinet. He held the salami in front of his own pants, pointing it upwards like a giant penis. "Hey, it'd be nice to have this, huh?" Everyone laughed—except Marco, who exhaled deeply and closed his eyes.

"I said, grab your ankles!" said Sal.

The other men pushed Marco's torso down and began duct-taping his hands to his ankles. By now Marco was sobbing convulsively, and he screamed hideously as they tried to push the salami into his ass.

"Gag this piece of shit!" said Sal. The meat market was in a small strip mall, with all the businesses connected, and people in the other shops might be able to hear what was going on. One of the men grabbed a bloody meat rag that had been used to clean the counter. It was covered with tiny scraps of meat and fat. They crammed it into Marco's mouth until none of the rag was showing, then wrapped duct tape around and around his head to keep it in place. After pushing for several minutes, the salami was still protruding almost a foot, so one of the men picked up a metal snow shovel leaning against the wall next to the door and started pounding the salami into Marco, slamming the shovel against it again and again and again—*clang! clang! clang!*—until less than an inch of the salami showed. They finally let Marco drop to the floor and stepped aside.

As they were leaving, Al noticed a slow-cooker full of hot meatballs stewing on the counter. "Hey, any you guys want a meatball sub?" He took a long hoagie roll from a plastic bag, made a slit down the side with a knife, then piled on the meatballs, sauce, and mozzarella. Cutting it in two, he gave half to Sal. They were munching on the subs as everyone walked from the shop, while Marco lay on the floor behind the counter, his muffled groans barely audible.

"They left him there like that, gagged and duct-taped, with a salami stuck in his ass," said Greg. "Probably did all kinds of internal damage. It was horrible to watch. My dad made me go along. He was brutal. We got in the car, you know, and I never bet with a bookie again."

BUSTED

Greg was sitting at the kitchen table of his family's home eating a bowl of cereal when he heard the knock at the front door. Thinking nothing of it, he got up and turned the knob. Wham! The door flung open, and several burly FBI agents and SWAT team police burst inside, wearing full body armor and wielding machine guns. "Get on the floor now! Now!" they shouted, one of them pointing a machine gun in his face, while another grabbed him and threw him face-down on the living room floor. "Don't move!"

Simultaneously, other cops were coming in from the back door and the basement windows, streaming in through every possible entrance to the house.

"Is there anyone else here?" one asked.

"Yeah, just my father," said Greg.

"They grabbed him like two seconds later," Greg told me. "He was lying in bed in the room where he took all his bets—the room where he 'took his action,' as he called it."

They laid Herb face-down right beside Greg on the old shag carpet, and it stunk. Herb glanced over at Greg, who looked terrified. He was still just a high school student, a few months from graduating. Although Herb was in pain and twitching noticeably from his Parkinson's disease, he smiled broadly at his son.

"He was looking right at me and said, 'You know, that's where Ollie [one of their dogs] took a shit this morning.' We both started laughing. And the cops were looking at us like, 'What the fuck are you guys laughing about when you're under arrest?' That's the way he was. He didn't want me to freak out."

One of the people involved in the raid was a state policeman, and when things settled down he let them get up from the floor. Greg went into the kitchen with him. The policeman recognized Greg.

"You're a great football player," he said. "I was at the championship game. My next-door neighbor is the head coach at Middletown, and he says you're one of the greatest players he ever played against."

"Wow, thank you," said Greg. "That's really an honor."

After some small talk about where Greg might go to college and what he intended to do in the future, Greg asked if they needed him for anything else.

"No, we're just going to take pictures of every room in the house," said the policeman.

Greg cringed, remembering the six-foot-tall marijuana plant he'd been growing in his bedroom window all winter. As soon as he could slip away, he went upstairs and moved the plant behind a bookcase, but it was so large, part of it stuck out over the top. After telling the policeman he was going to take off now, Greg walked to the house of a neighbor who had been involved with Herb in his bookie operation, hoping to warn him. But it was too late—he was already being led away in handcuffs. Greg slipped into the woods and hid out for a few hours, waiting for things to settle down.

The next time Greg saw his father, Herb laughed and said, "Thanks a lot. Not only did I get arrested for several racketeering charges but also possession and cultivation of marijuana!"

"My father took all the charges," said Greg. Some thirty mobsters in all were arrested in the roundup, many of them far worse criminals than Herb: mob bosses and enforcers.

"Some of them went to prison forever," said Greg. But the court was lenient with Herb. "His Parkinson's was really getting advanced by that time. They brought him into court in a wheelchair, and the state didn't want to deal with it. I don't think they really wanted to put him in prison. They just put him on probation for five years, and that was that."

HERB'S ILLNESS

Herb's physical condition was deteriorating fast. When he had first shown signs of Parkinson's disease in his early forties, when Greg was twelve, it had come on gradually and was barely noticeable—some stiffness in his leg, a slight limp—so he was still fully able to run his bookie operation and to punish people who crossed him. But by the time Greg was in his late teens, Herb's illness had progressed to the point that he twitched constantly and had a hard time doing the most basic physical activities. He was so desperate for relief that he volunteered to take part in experimental surgery and was one of the first people to have fetal tissue implanted in his brain. At first, the procedure seemed successful. Herb was awake when Greg went to visit him and seemed noticeably better.

"He was just sitting there with his head completely wrapped in bandages, but for the first time in quite a while he was calm," said Greg. "Normally, he would have been all over the place, twitching, flailing around."

But the positive effects didn't last, and his symptoms came back stronger than ever. It wasn't easy for Herb—or for Greg. One day he got so frustrated when he was visiting his father in the hospital, he threatened to throw the doctor out the sixth-floor window. The man called security, and two policemen came and stood guard outside Herb's room while Greg visited.

Herb was losing everything. He couldn't take bets anymore, and several people who owed him money were ignoring his requests to be paid. Greg heard about one man who owed Herb $15,000 and was bragging to people that he wasn't going to pay. "What's he going to do to make me?" the man had said. Greg exploded when he heard that and paid the man a visit. Herb got his money a short time later. He knew nothing about what Greg had done.

"I put the fear of Jesus in a few of those people back then," said Greg. "They thought I was crazy and might do anything."

Despite Greg's efforts, Herb no longer had an income. All they had was the money Diane made from teaching. They had to sell the house in North Haven, where Greg had grown up. It was a heartbreaker for everyone. They moved into a much smaller place, a condominium in another part of town.

Herb lived in the basement, in a space they fixed up to accommodate his handicap. By then, he needed to sit in a special chair that would raise him into a standing position at the touch of a button. That was the only way he could get on his feet. But walking was a struggle because of his constant shaking.

Then some of the medication he was taking started making him hallucinate. He frequently thought people were trying to attack him. He kept a pistol next to his bed, and sometimes when he got scared, he'd shoot off rounds, blasting gaping holes in the walls of the condo.

"The cops would always come," said Greg. "They'd take him to the hospital. I rode in the ambulance with him a few times. The worst time was the day of the Super Bowl. He was downstairs alone while we were watching the game upstairs, and he fired five shots." The police finally took away all of his guns.

The emotional toll was heavy on Greg. At this point, his brother

Dave was a Yale student and star pitcher on the university's baseball team and didn't come home much. (Herb had encouraged him to get away from all this and pursue his own life—first at Yale and then as an officer in the Marine Corps.) And Diane was emotionally checked out. A nurse took care of Herb, who spent most days smoking cigarettes and staring out the window as the television droned endlessly in the background.

At first Herb had been hopeful about his life. Maybe things would improve for him, he thought. But after the failed surgery and the side effects from the medication, he became deeply depressed. He felt his life was over and he would be better off dead.

Between his father's depression and his mother's raging mood swings, Greg couldn't stand to be at home. He spent more and more time fishing, going far out into Long Island Sound in pursuit of striped bass. He felt such a strong need to be out there—he could face any hardship, endure any setback, as long as he could get out on the water. He was still using the old Brockway he'd bought as a child. The years were taking a toll on the craft and it was leaking badly, but he refused to let the boat's condition limit him. He kept a small plastic bucket inside and bailed the water out whenever it got to be ankle deep.

On a perfect fishing day in late summer, Greg motored out to the Race, just as he'd done so many times before, ever since he was ten years old. He had all of his bass rods and lures with him and planned to spend the day fishing there alone. But just as he came within sight of Race Rock, he suddenly felt cold water rushing up past his ankles. The planks of the boat's hull were coming apart, and in seconds it started going under. Luckily, a couple of men in a nearby sport-fishing boat saw what was happening and quickly motored over to him. He handed them his best rod and reel, and then tried to save the outboard motor, unscrewing the clamp and hoisting it up from the transom at the rear of the boat, which was still above water. But the motor slipped from his grasp and quickly sank to the bottom. So Greg's trusty old boat, his motor, and all of his bass-fishing equipment except one rod and reel were lost.

As the other fishermen motored away with him, Greg sat in shock, drenched to the skin, gazing sadly back to where his old Brockway had been cruising through the chop less than an hour earlier. A flood of memories came rushing back to him—all the great things he had done with that boat; all the places he'd been; all the mighty striped bass he'd fought and landed with it. Was it really over? How would he ever be able to get by? The near-daily trips on his boat were such an essential escape valve for him, the only time he felt truly alive and free. Sure, he could scrounge rides with his friends on fishing boats, but it wouldn't be the same. He craved being able to go out fishing alone whenever things were bothering him, and that avenue was now closed to him, just when he needed it most.

"I immediately started thinking, *How am I going to get back on the water?*" said Greg. "*Because I need to be there; I need to be on the water.*" The thought of being stranded on land filled him with anxiety.

The fishermen who rescued him didn't want to go back to the harbor right away, so Greg spent the day in his wet clothes, fishing with them. They finally took him ashore at Groton, Connecticut. One of the men had to drive near Greg's house, so he dropped him off there.

Greg didn't tell his parents anything about what happened that day. Losing his boat was such a profound shock, he didn't know what to say, and the situation with his father made everything more difficult. Herb had recently started begging Greg to take his life. "Every time I saw him, he was asking me to kill him," he said. "It was a painful time."

As his father became more and more ill, Greg's tension increased markedly, and after losing his boat, he no longer had a constructive way to deal with his anxiety. He began drinking heavily, often putting away a liter of Jim Beam or Tanqueray a night, and abusing a variety of drugs: cocaine, barbiturates, and amphetamines. He was still underage, only eighteen years old, but he would sit at the local bar drinking, and no one dared ask him for his ID. Something had changed in him.

"I used to be someone who really never wanted to fight anyone— someone who didn't even like confrontation," said Greg. "I was more into fishing and trapping and spending as much time as I could out in the woods."

Then one day, as he sat quietly drinking alone in the bar, an old nemesis of Greg's walked in. He was a couple of years older than Greg and had tormented him mercilessly in junior high, sometimes slapping him hard in the face as they passed in the hallway, just for the hell of it. He was a huge man now and worked in a factory in New Haven. His shift had just ended and he'd stopped at the bar for a drink. Without being asked, the bartender gave him a double Scotch, which he downed instantly, then slammed the glass back down on the bar and nodded for the bartender to fill it again. He was drinking his second Scotch when he happened to glance at Greg, sitting three stools down from him at the bar.

"Oh, fuck! Is that you?" he said. "Little Greggie?" And he slapped Greg hard, right in the face. "Just like old times, huh?"

Greg felt an unstoppable rage coursing through his body and punched the man as hard as he could, landing a devastating blow to his face, followed by another and another and another, pummeling him endlessly, breaking bones in his face, spattering blood and spit and snot everywhere until the man lay senseless on the barroom floor.

"That was the first time I ever snapped and started throwing punches like that," said Greg. "After that, I never had a fear about fighting anyone." At that instant, Greg had become his father's son.

THE PHANTOM

Greg was an All-State and All-American football player in high school, and after his stunning performance in the championship game, many major college athletic programs aggressively courted him. One coach even bribed Scott Jackson to try to talk Greg into taking the full-ride scholarship deal they were offering at their university. Scott happily took the money and spent it with Greg.

Dave Myerson remembers the phone calls well. "Once I was in the house and the phone rang, and it was Johnny Majors, the head coach at Tennessee at the time, and he was calling because they were trying to recruit my brother."

During his final semester of high school, Greg was often called up to the office to take a call from some college or other that wanted him on their team. The administrators and faculty at Lyman Hall High School were very supportive, excited that one of their students had such a great opportunity before him. But Greg took advantage of them. On the days he went to the office to take a phone call, he would often just leave school, skipping the rest of the day instead of going back to his classes.

Greg turned down some of the top colleges in the country and chose instead to attend the University of Rhode Island. Some people, like his brother Dave, were surprised he took their scholarship offer instead of going with one of the powerhouse schools that were courting him.

"He had Tennessee, Penn State, and these other great schools interested in him, and he opted for Rhode Island," said Dave. "It was a surprise for me, but I know he was always more comfortable with URI. It was closer to home, and it was a place where he could fish for striped bass—which is actually what probably drove it all."

Greg agrees with Dave's assessment. Although he did have a guarantee from URI that he would be a starter in his first year, what really clinched the deal was the school's close proximity to excellent striped bass fishing.

But Greg's time at the University of Rhode Island didn't start well. Even before the semester began, he had a bad experience at the end of the summer football training camp. The new recruits were staying in a dormitory on campus, and on Rookie Night, the last night of camp, everyone in the football program got dressed up and went to the Galley Beach Club for dinner. Afterward, the seniors put the new recruits through hazing hell, screaming at them, stripping them naked, hitting them with paddles, then locking them all up in a bathroom in the dark. Then they took them out one by one and made them stand under a single light bulb as they taunted and humiliated them. Each of them had to put an act on in front of the team, trying to entertain them and make them laugh. Regardless of what they did, each freshman met with the same fate: the seniors pelted them with a sticky, disgusting substance they'd mixed together.

"It was some revolting blend of rotten eggs, molasses, and maybe piss, shit, tobacco spit, tomatoes—whatever they could find—whipped together into a stinking mess," said Greg.

When it was his turn, he was defiant. He flipped them off and yelled, "Fuck you!" Someone instantly smashed him just above his eye with a rotten egg, and his head swelled up.

"Over my eye, I had a big welt. Then they started pelting me with that sticky stuff."

When it was over, all twelve of them knelt on the ground, six on each side, facing each other, covered in gooey brown goop—but their initiation was over. By that time, Greg had had it. He just wanted to get out of there and drive nonstop all the way home. He tried to wipe off the sticky goop, but it was hopeless. He couldn't even put his clothes on, so he gathered them up in a bundle, walked out to his pickup truck, and sped away buck-naked into the night.

Greg was driving close to ninety miles an hour when a state trooper pulled him over. It was nearly midnight. The trooper walked up to his truck and shone a flashlight inside, illuminating Greg's naked, goop-smeared body.

"You been drinking?" he asked.

"No, I just had the worst fucking night of my life."

"Yeah, well why don't you tell me about it?"

And Greg proceeded to lay out the events of the evening in exacting detail. The trooper was silent for a few seconds, and Greg couldn't see his face. "You're going to have to wait here a minute," he finally said and walked back to his squad car. Several minutes later another state trooper drove up—and then another . . . and another . . . and another.

"They all walked up to my truck, and I was sitting there, looking straight ahead," said Greg. "They've got flashlights shining on me. I've got shit in my hair . . . shit all over me. And they're fucking laughing at me. I'm like, 'Yeah, yeah, yeah; very funny.' And they're like, 'All right, get the fuck out of here.'"

When Greg got home, Herb did his best to help him wash, limping outside with a bucket, a bar of soap, and a brush, and holding a garden hose over Greg as he knelt in the yard, trying to scrub himself clean. He scoured himself until he bled, but it was hopeless.

"I don't even know what it was, but I couldn't get it off," he said. "I finally had to shave my head." He was furious with his teammates.

"After that, I was on a rampage of terror, taking them all out, one at a time, in practice. I was brutal. They were very afraid."

When Greg moved into his URI dormitory a couple weeks later, things didn't go much better. Scott Jackson drove him there in his pickup truck, and he had a beer keg in back with a tube running into the cab that they could drink from. By the time they reached URI, Greg was so drunk he could barely walk. He staggered into his dorm and sprawled out on the first bed he came to. Scott carried all of Greg's things into the dorm, left them stacked beside the bed, and drove back to Connecticut without another word.

When the semester started, Greg rarely showed up at classes and sometimes even missed team practice. He spent most days fishing and most nights drinking, smoking pot, or snorting coke. The head coach started calling him the Phantom, because he never knew where he was and when he might show up. One day the coach was sitting on the sea-wall at Narragansett Beach, drinking a cup of coffee, when he noticed Greg standing in the surf with his fishing rod, casting again and again into the surging water. Later, at practice, the coach confronted him about it.

"How were your classes today?" he asked.

"Oh, pretty good," said Greg. "Normal stuff."

"Yeah, well, I saw you fishing all day at Narragansett. I watched you."

From then on, the coach sent two huge football players to wake Greg up every morning, go to breakfast with him, and escort him to his first class.

"It did help," said Greg. "But a lot of times, if the fishing was good, I'd go to the first class and then take off."

Still, Greg was an excellent football player, and that mitigated a lot of his problems with the coaching staff. In one of his first games for URI, he made one of the best plays of his entire football career. The other team was about to punt on a third down, and Greg went in for the block, leapt right over the center the instant the ball was hiked, and dashed toward the punter.

"There were two guys in front of the punter, and I lowered down like I was going to hit them," said Greg. "But instead, I jumped over them and blocked the punt." In doing so, Greg flipped over in the air and landed on his back with the wind knocked out of him. But URI had possession of the ball on the other team's twenty-yard line, and they scored on the next play.

One of Greg's first close friendships at URI was with Bear Judkins, another player on the varsity football team. But they didn't hit it off so well at the start.

"We first met at rookie orientation for football at URI, and I hated him," said Bear. "I just thought he was obnoxious and arrogant, and I didn't like him at all. Then one day he opened up to me, and we started becoming friends. He told me lots of stories about when he was growing up, and about his father, who was a gangster, but when I met him he had Parkinson's disease and was pretty sick."

Greg and Bear started working out together and had their own running route they went on several times a week. They would take fishing rods with them and run along the Rhode Island shoreline from the Coast Guard House Restaurant in Narragansett Beach all the way down around Hazard Rock and Black Point to Scarborough Beach, racing each other across boulders and climbing up rocky outcroppings until they couldn't run another step, while the waves pounded relentlessly beside them, splashing up and covering them with salt spray. Then they'd stop and fish for a while until they were rested enough to run again.

THE RATTLER

In the summer after his first year at the University of Rhode Island, when he was nineteen, Greg went home to his parents' condo and started working for an electrical contractor who did a lot of jobs at Yale University. Greg's uncle, an electrical union foreman, had helped him get hired, and he was perfect for the job. He knew where everything was located on campus because of all the time he'd spent there in high school, hanging around with his brother Dave and his friends, so the company hired him to make deliveries to their various work sites and to do other odd jobs around the shop.

The company was in a particularly bad part of New Haven, wracked by gang violence and drug abuse—mostly crack cocaine, which was then reaching epidemic levels. It was a grim place. Greg often felt as though he was traveling through a war zone as he drove to and from the shop; shootings and stabbings were commonplace, and a couple of times people threw bricks at his windshield when he passed. Each morning, one of his first tasks was to sweep up all the empty crack vials that accumulated every night in the parking lot. But doing this kind of mindless work gave Greg plenty of time to think. It was here that he first began experimenting with the idea of creating a sound-producing sinker.

Greg had already been dissecting the stomachs of the large striped bass he was catching, trying to find out exactly what they were eating. He discovered that the largest bass were often feeding on lobsters—and suddenly it all made sense. A bass would have to be of a certain size to have jaws strong enough to crunch through the tough lobster shells; smaller bass simply were not big enough to eat them. This was great to know, but how could he use it to catch these giant bass? He became obsessed with finding the answer.

He wondered how the fish found the lobsters. The kinds of places lobsters frequent tend to have poor visibility, so he doubted they could spot them by eye. And the fish's sense of smell probably wouldn't be sufficient to find them in the churning waters surrounding reefs, jetties, and rocky shorelines. Could it be that the stripers heard the rattle of the lobsters' carapaces as they shuffled across the rocks, foraging for food?

To find out, Greg set up a 200-gallon saltwater fish tank with a granite bottom in the living room and released several live lobsters in it that he'd bought at a fish market. He would sit beside the aquarium for hours with a medical stethoscope pressed tightly against the glass, listening intently to the sounds of the lobsters. He found that whenever they moved, their carapaces would make a clicking or rattling sound. It finally dawned on him what he needed to do—he would figure out a way to mimic that sound, which would attract only fish large enough to eat lobsters, just the bass he most wanted to catch. But would any kind of rattling noise do? Greg had his doubts, so he bought an acoustic-metering device, which enabled him to determine the exact frequency and decibel level of the sounds.

Greg knew that the idea of using sound to attract big stripers had a lot of merit, if he could just figure out how to do it. He thought about it a lot while he was at work. One morning, as he was sweeping up crack vials, he had a revelation. What if he put tiny ball bearings inside the glass vials to create miniature rattles? He set out immediately to see if it would work. First he cleaned the vials out thoroughly with Q-tips, then he filled them with ball bearings of varying sizes and shapes. He then rattled them underwater to see which ones worked best.

Fortunately, Greg had become good friends with his boss, Joe, who allowed him to work on his own projects when business was slow at the shop. So Greg experimented with the rattle vials almost every day. After determining the best size and configuration of ball bearings to use in the vials to re-create the sounds of lobsters, Greg figured he could attach them to the end of his fishing line to use as a sound-producing sinker. But there was a problem: the glass vials would quickly get broken on the rocks. His solution was to get a large lead fishing sinker, bore a hole in it big enough to accommodate a crack vial, slip the vial inside, and cover it up with lead.

"We had a drill press in the back of the shop," said Greg. "I built a wooden jig to hold the sinker in place while I drilled a hole in it the perfect size for a crack vial. I'd put ball bearings into the vial, then slip it into the sinker and tamp lead over it. You couldn't even see it. My sinker looked like everyone else's, except mine made a clicking noise."

So someone looking in Greg's tackle box wouldn't even know there was anything special in there—which was a crucial consideration. Greg had recently started going on nighttime fishing trips with a couple other electricians who worked for the company. He had borrowed a boat from his old friends, the Carlsons, and he and the others would take it out in Long Island Sound almost every night, sometimes going all the way to Block Island and sleeping there in the boat. They were very competitive, always trying to outdo each other in fishing. Often they would bet to see who would catch the biggest or most fish, which gave Greg a great incentive to work on his rattle sinker. He was convinced it would give him an unbeatable edge.

"At night we would go fishing in deep water for striped bass using a three-way technique like I do now," said Greg. "But I was trying to figure out how to get the fish to come to my bait and not my friends' bait. I figured it had to be noise, but it couldn't be noticeable."

The three-way technique employs a three-way swivel tied at the end of the fishing line. One of the eyes of the swivel is attached to a couple of feet of leader with the hook and bait at the end. The third eye is attached to another leader with a heavy—three- to six-ounce—sinker at the end to pull the rig down to the bottom during a running tide. Greg honed and perfected the technique to fit his needs. He found that if he dropped his rig right down to the reef far below his boat and walked it slowly and gently along the rocks as the boat drifted, he could almost perfectly mimic the sound and behavior of a lobster, and thus attract the biggest bass. But could he catch them? Just because you lure them in with a strange noise doesn't necessarily mean they'll bite. Greg started hooking an eel on a short line a few inches from the rattle.

"I know as soon as they're close enough to the rattle to hit it, they're going to smell the eel, because they hunt by hearing first and then by smell," said Greg. "The trick is to get them to think there's a lobster in the area." (Using a rattle sinker and eel is actually much better than even using a live lobster, which would be prohibitively expensive, only good for one or two drifts, and not as effective. A rattle sinker dangling a foot above the rocks sends out a better sound signal than a real lobster would, because it mimics the sound of a lobster moving through the rocks without *being* in the rocks.)

Greg didn't stop there. He experimented with different kinds of fishing line and eventually changed from using monofilament, which most striper fishermen use, to a braided line.

"There's a lot of stretch in monofilament, so you can't detect the little hits made by stripers," said Greg. "With the braided line, I can feel it even if a fish just swims past my line. Any little bump, and I know a fish is close by. A lot of times they hit the rattle sinker just because they don't know what it is. And then they smell the eel."

He also began working to develop a fishing rod that would be more sensitive and effective to use with his walking technique. First he shortened the rod and put a roller at the tip instead of the usual solid-metal guide. Braided line pulled taut by a big fish fighting to escape can be very abrasive to the metal guide at the rod tip, and a roller helps prevent excessive wear. Then he added more line guides to the rod, spacing them more closely. And he began using the old-style cork handles instead of the new foam plastic ones, because he found them more comfortable to use on a long night of fishing. (Years later, after he had caught the world-record striper, he designed a line of Greg Myerson signature rods for Lamiglas Fishing Rods, incorporating all of these design elements.)

One thing that has always fascinated Greg about the striped bass is that it has personality. It is very curious. Divers who have watched these and other fish underwater have noted the differences in the behavior of various species. Bluefish and many other fish species take off immediately if they see a diver. But a striped bass will come up and investigate to see what the diver is. Some researchers have been able to hand-feed large wild stripers, tossing out chunks of lobster to them.

"I use their curiosity to catch them," said Greg. The sound made by his rattling sinkers piques their interest. They will sometimes smash into one of his sinkers or swim by quickly, swooshing past the fishing line. "I can almost predict exactly when they will hit the bait," he said.

Greg's invention worked better than he could ever have imagined. After he started using his crack-vial rattle sinker, he pulled out ahead of the other fishermen and never looked back. Fishing in ninety feet of water at night, in the dark, he was catching twelve stripers for each one the others caught.

"My sinker looked like everyone else's except mine made a clicking noise," he said. "And I started catching really, really big fish. It was my secret weapon."

Before long, his friends stopped betting with him, so he started going out on big sport-fishing charter boats, the kind that can carry a hundred anglers. Most of the fishermen on the boats would put money in a betting pool, where the person who catches the biggest fish gets all the money. It became a big hustle for him. Greg won so often that people stopped putting money in the pool, or, in some cases, the captain of the boat wouldn't let him compete in it.

This was when Greg truly honed his skills and fully developed the concept of the rattle sinker, from the time he was a college student and into his twenties after he left school. For years, he didn't tell anyone how he was catching so many big fish—not until after he'd caught the world-record striped bass and decided to launch a company to manufacture and sell his invention to other anglers.

In addition to developing the rattle sinker, designing more effective rods, and improving striped bass fishing techniques, Greg studied the tides and the cycles of the moon—anything to give him an edge in his fishing. He noticed that the tides move very fast during new moons and full moons, making them a less desirable time to fish.

"At those times, the tide starts ripping so fast—three, four, or five knots [one knot equals 1.15 miles per hour]—you can't even fish," said Greg. "It's not a good time for anything. A lobster can't feed when the water's rushing past at five knots."

In Greg's opinion, the best time to fish is during the first-quarter moon. "It's a slow tide, with the moon dead high in the sky at sunset," he said. "For a lot of the evening, the moon is right overhead, while the water is moving slowly and the lobsters are feeding. When the tide is changing, the water is almost completely still. You can almost fish the entire tide, and the water is never moving more than two knots."

With all his years of experience in the waters of Long Island Sound, Greg could see how connected everything is in that vast ecosystem. As early as his late teens, he'd already been out there in every month, at all times of day and night, and in almost every possible weather condition, even when he had no business risking his life there. He knew the effects of the moon, the tide, and the seasons at an intuitive level, and he knew exactly when he'd have the best chance to catch the biggest fish.

WILD MAN

Greg was living in a frat house made up mostly of football players. One Saturday night in early January, the frat house next door—where around a hundred students lived, most of whom disliked football players—was having a huge keg party. Its downstairs bar was packed with dozens of people, all drinking and partying. Greg's frat house was fairly quiet by comparison, with fifteen or twenty people hanging around, drinking and smoking pot. Greg had already downed most of a bottle of Tanqueray gin and popped several codeine pills he'd stolen from the football trainer's office. He was feeling no pain.

Tyrone, an African American student who was on the URI basketball team, showed up and said they should try to crash the party next door. Most of them didn't want any part of it, but Greg was all in. He, Tyrone, and a couple others walked next door. A security guard stood at the entrance, while several large frat men were just inside, one of them drinking Jack Daniel's from a bottle. Greg and his friends started to push their way inside.

"Hey, you can't come in here," said the guy with the whiskey bottle, and the guard and the other students standing nearby backed him up. Greg smirked and walked back outside. Determined to get into the party, he and Tyrone went around back to the fire escape, climbed up to the third story, and forced a door open. Greg took off his white ski jacket before walking downstairs, hoping no one would recognize him, but one of the men standing at the front door spotted him instantly. Grabbing Greg by the throat, he dragged him to the door. "Get out of here!" he yelled as he pushed him outside, but Greg got hold of the man's collar and yanked as hard as he could, and they both fell off the porch into the snow. Greg was on him immediately, raining punches in his face. The man with the whiskey bottle, standing nearby, smashed the bottle right in Greg's face, slashing his nose wide open. Greg didn't feel anything. He stood up and landed a crushing blow to the man's face, dropping him to the ground, and then everyone came surging out and lunging at him, trying to punch or kick him.

"Ten, twenty, thirty—I have no idea how many," said Greg. "And they were all trying to get a piece of me. I was so stoned, I didn't feel anything."

Tyrone ran next door to get help, so Greg stood alone, facing a horde of angry frat boys. And he took them all on, throwing round-house kicks, swinging and punching, landing devastating blows. He finally made a break for it, trying to get back to his own frat house, but he was tackled in the parking lot. They were all kicking Greg as he lay there trying to cover himself from their attack.

"Hey, that's enough," said one of his attackers. "We'll kill him if we don't stop." Then Greg got back on his feet and punched one of them in the face as hard as he could, and the whole thing started over, with everyone raining down punches and kicks on Greg and dragging him to the ground again.

The town police from Kingston, Rhode Island, finally showed up and separated everyone. Greg stood back up, his face bruised and bleeding profusely from his slashed nose, his shirt ripped to shreds. There was blood everywhere—his own as well as the blood of the people he'd hit. The police were holding back the crowd. "All right, all right, that's enough," they barked. "Everyone back off!"

Greg was in a strange daze. He barely knew what was going on around him, but he had no intention of quitting. He suddenly ran at the crowd full speed with his fist cocked up. "I remember seeing this one big guy's face, and it's like he's thinking, 'Holy shit! He's going to hit me.' And *bang!* I punched him in the mouth so hard he fell back ten steps."

The crowd erupted instantly, shouting, "Kill him! Kill him!" and pushing through the police line. Greg made a break for it again and ran past his frat house, where all the football players lived. And everyone came running out, wearing football and hockey helmets, many of them carrying hockey sticks, lacrosse sticks, and whatever else they could grab. A huge brawl ensued, and the police couldn't stop it.

As the fight went on all around him, Greg was lying over a sewer grate, listening to the sound of his blood dripping down into the water. His friends finally picked him up off the ground and took him to the student infirmary. The place was overwhelmed as a dozen or more badly beaten students showed up, one after another. Some of them, including Greg, needed surgery. Ambulances arrived and took the most seriously injured students to nearby South County Hospital. The emergency room looked like a disaster zone, with bruised and bleeding frat boys on every available bed or gurney. Greg was on a table getting stitches in his nose. The guy on the next table was the one he had run over to and smashed in the mouth as the police held everyone back. Both his upper and lower lips were split open and a surgeon was sewing them up. The guy turned to Greg and said, "What the fuck did you do this to me for?"

"Well, you shouldn't have been outside, you fat fuck!" said Greg.

"You're dead, Myerson. You're fucking dead!"

Greg broke away from the doctor who was sewing him up and started punching the other man in the face until his stitches opened up and his lips were bleeding profusely again. The state police came rushing into the emergency room and put handcuffs on Greg, which he wore through the rest of his surgery.

The fight was covered in both the *Providence Journal* and the student newspaper, *The Cigar*. The headline read: "Greek Misunderstanding Sends 10 to the Hospital."

After the night of the brawl, people at URI viewed Greg differently, and no one wanted to mess with him. "I was well known on campus, and feared after that by everyone," said Greg. "I wasn't a bad dude, I just wouldn't take any kind of crap."

The police and the campus blamed Greg for the brawl, and he was put on probation at the university. As punishment, the director of Campus Life required him to drive the handicapped van around campus, but Greg came to enjoy spending time with the students he drove.

"There were all these students in wheelchairs—paraplegics—and I would visit them in their dorm rooms," said Greg. "They loved me because I'd come walking in with football players, and we'd smoke weed with them and bring them to places with us. We became friends. They were good people."

Greg's time at the University of Rhode Island did not end the way he had hoped, with a bachelor's degree and a spot on an NFL team. He was an amazing football player, as anyone who ever saw him on the field can attest, but the academics—and the drugs and alcohol—did him in. His heart was just never in it, and at the end of his sophomore year of college, he was on the ropes. Late in that second year he tried to turn it around. He managed to get his grades up in a couple of classes, but he needed one professor to give him an incomplete instead of an F to be able to keep his athletic scholarship. He explained the situation to the professor and said that he'd had three surgeries on his nose that semester (thanks to the brawl) and had gotten behind in his work.

"You should have come to me earlier," he told Greg. "There's nothing I can do now. But if you get an A on your final, you'll pass the course."

Greg knew there was no way he could ever get an A on his exam, so he implored the professor to reconsider. "Look, I really need this incomplete."

"Maybe you should just go home and bag groceries for a while and figure out what you want to do with your life," he said.

"I wanted to kill that guy," said Greg. "But he was right. I didn't know what I wanted. I was at URI for two years, and then it was over, along with any chance I had of ever playing in the NFL."

RASTA MON

Greg was at loose ends when he left the University of Rhode Island. He couldn't stand being stuck at his parents' condo. His father was sicker than ever and kept begging Greg to put him out of his misery; and his mother was furious with him for dropping out of college and scolded him constantly. "Why can't you be more like Dave?" she fumed. Even when she didn't say anything, Greg knew exactly what she was thinking, and it made being there a nightmare.

He drove his Jeep to a vegetable farm not far from home to try to get a job. With his background in the vo-ag program at Lyman Hall High School and his previous work on farms, he was an instant hire. He worked alongside nearly two dozen Jamaicans, who would come to this area for a few months each year as migrant farm laborers, then go back home with the money they'd earned. The wages were much better in the United States than what they could earn in Jamaica, and many farm owners considered them the most skilled, efficient, and hardworking farm help they could find anywhere.

Greg was a hard worker and was put in charge of one of the two crews of ten Jamaicans. The Jamaicans loved Greg, because they knew he respected them. He had been growing marijuana at home in his closet, using a grow light, and he had a good-sized stash of it. He would bring a bag of it each day to share with them, and they would smoke it together whenever they took a break. The other crew didn't get to do this. For the Jamaicans, this fit right in with their lifestyle at home, and they worked all the harder for Greg. He was the perfect boss man for them. Their output was amazing; they were picking nearly twice as much as the other crew.

Greg enjoyed working with the Jamaicans. He admired their easygoing worldview; nothing fazed them. They were so close-knit, friendly, and generous—and they had such a great dialect. Greg was soon speaking just like them, which endeared him to them even more.

One of Greg's favorite workers at the orchard was Winston, a stocky, six-foot-five, middle-aged Jamaican whom the others on the crew called the "Long Man." At the end of the harvest, when the last of the crops had been picked, Winston invited Greg to come and visit him at his home in the mountains of Jamaica, and Greg said he definitely would. He started making arrangements, getting a passport and a one-way ticket to Kingston, the capital city of Jamaica. Greg wasn't sure how long he was going to stay, perhaps only a week or two, but he figured he could just buy a return ticket whenever he decided to come home.

Greg arrived at Kingston airport with the clothes on his back, $300 in his pocket, and a backpack with a few additional items of clothing. He had only a vague idea of where he was going. Winston had told him to get a cab and tell the driver to take him to an area in the mountains, about twenty miles from Kingston, and ask around for him. He followed Winston's instructions, but the cab driver seemed shocked when Greg told him where he was going. "Why you wanna go there, mon?" he asked, gazing quizzically at him in the rearview mirror. But he went ahead and drove him there. As they got higher into the mountains, the road became ever more treacherous—muddy and washed out in places. The driver finally said he could go no farther in his battered old Ford station wagon. So he pointed the way to Greg, collected his fare, and wished him well.

Greg still had five or six miles to go, but he had a strange sensation he was being followed. He kept catching glimpses of a couple of men walking behind him, but whenever he looked back toward them, they would duck quickly into the trees and undergrowth and hide. Then he didn't see them for a while, until suddenly they jumped out ahead of him in the trail, wielding machetes threateningly. Somehow they had made their way around him through the woods and gotten out in front. They took his backpack, which contained his passport and other identification, his clothes, and all of his money. They even took his shoes and the shirt off his back. Greg was barefoot and clad only in cutoff shorts when he found Winston a couple of hours later. The Long Man welcomed him warmly, laughing heartily and hugging him like a long-lost brother.

Winston lived in a small two-bedroom wooden house—just a shack, really, like something from the 1960s television show *Gilligan's Island*, cobbled together from various planks, two-by-fours, and other building materials he'd acquired over the years. Winston was considered better off than most of the other people in the village because of the farm work he did each year in the United States, but his house was little more than a hovel. Still, Greg was happy to have a room of his own in such a beautiful place.

Winston shook his head and laughed when he heard about Greg's robbery. He didn't seem surprised. He pulled out a bag of marijuana, then quickly rolled a joint and handed it to Greg, who lit it up and took a long, deep drag, holding the smoke in as long as he could, finally releasing it in a massive gray cloud. He took another hit and handed the joint back to Winston. Greg smiled. Things didn't seem so bad after all. It was warm and sunny and pleasant here, and it was good to be with Winston again; he had such an infectious sense of humor and happiness.

Soon other people from the village started showing up at Winston's shack. They'd all heard about Greg and were eager to meet him. They crowded around him, laughing till tears filled their eyes as he spoke the local vernacular like a Jamaican. Several people went home and brought back logs and lit a fire. Some brought food, including fruits and vegetables and a huge pot of curried goat, which they put on the fire. Before long, the little get-together had developed into a full-on party, with every man, woman, and child in the village taking part. And everyone — including Greg — laughed and sang and danced long into the night.

Greg quickly got into the groove of living in Jamaica. He had originally thought he would spend only a week or so there at the most, but things were so easy and mellow, his time away stretched into two weeks, then three, and he still hadn't made arrangements to get back home. And why should he? He wasn't at all eager to return to the specter of his father wasting slowly away and the rage of his mother. Besides, it was going to be a hassle to get his paperwork straightened out so he could get home. He'd have to go back to Kingston without any money and throw himself on the mercy of the American Embassy to help him get back to the United States. And Jamaica was so nice. Greg was having a great time with Winston and all his other new friends, living just like a Jamaican and loving it — eating the amazing food; working in the fields with the other men, whacking away at sugarcane with a machete and tying it in huge bundles; and getting lean and tan and strong, his hair bleached surfer blond by the Caribbean sun.

Greg went to church every Sunday with the Jamaicans in a simple wood-frame building that looked like an old one-room schoolhouse. The congregation was always enthusiastic. "The church service was just like a scene from *Forrest Gump* — lots of singing and dancing," said Greg. He was the only white person anywhere near, but the people completely embraced him. "I loved it there. I almost didn't ever want to leave."

Winston's shack stood on a hill, surrounded by coconut palms and other tropical vegetation. The weather was steadily pleasant — warm but with a cool breeze always blowing in from the ocean to keep the humidity down. It seemed as near to paradise as Greg could ever imagine. While he was staying there, he helped Winston make improvements to his house, such as wiring it up, making it one of the few dwellings in the village with electricity. They would sit together in the evening, smoking pot and listening to the radio. It was strange hearing the news of the world. It all seemed so distant and alien to Greg now. *This is the way life should be*, he thought, sitting sleepily on a porch, high on a hill in an island paradise.

One night the radio brought some disturbing news: a massive tropical storm was gathering strength in the Caribbean and would probably hit Jamaica within three days. It was hard to imagine. The weather had been sunny, clear, and pleasant for days and would remain that way right up to the morning when the storm arrived. The storm, dubbed Gilbert, would become a Category 3 hurricane by the time it hit Jamaica, the most damaging storm that had ever struck there in recorded history.

Greg and Winston went to each house in the village to alert people: "Batten down de hatches, mon. A storm be comin'." They hammered plywood boards across the windows in Winston's shack and helped others do the same to their dwellings; everyone brought as much of their outdoor belongings inside as they could fit. But after taking these precautions, Greg and Winston quickly got back into the relaxed Jamaican mode. They'd done all they could. Might as well kick back, smoke a joint, and enjoy the show when all hell broke loose on the island.

The clear blue skies that dawned three days later were deceptive. Maybe nothing would happen after all; it was so calm. But at midmorning, a dark, swirling maelstrom of pent-up energy began looming on the horizon, moving quickly closer, horrifying in its potential. Greg didn't know what to make of it. Even Winston had never seen anything like this in all his years there. As the storm broke, they went inside Winston's shack and hunkered down.

Winston still didn't seem fazed. He smiled, lit up another joint, and handed it to Greg. They sat smoking pot and munching on leftover food from the night before, feeling perfectly secure in the Long Man's wooden shack. Of course, the electricity went out the instant the high winds hit the island. That was to be expected. But the moaning of the wind and the way it kept picking up in intensity, getting louder and louder as it lashed the tiny village, quickly rising to a howling crescendo, was terrifying. Greg kept glancing over at Winston, trying to read his face, but he was as inscrutable as ever, smiling whenever Greg looked his way. *Maybe things will be okay*, Greg thought. *Maybe this is the way it always is when storms hit Jamaica.* But then the roof blew off the shack and the walls began tumbling down.

Greg and Winston fled outside. The wind, well over 100 miles an hour, instantly knocked them off their feet. They crawled on all fours to some nearby coconut palms and clung to them as tightly as barnacles on the hull of a boat. Greg assumed that this would last for ten or fifteen minutes, or maybe an hour at most, like a violent summer thunderstorm back home. But it continued, knocking over trees and houses all around them. Coconuts kept blowing past Greg like howitzer shells, exploding as they hit objects in their path, sending shrapnel-like fragments everywhere. He struggled to keep his head down. Several coconuts hit his body, and it felt like getting struck by huge rocks. His shoulder—the one he'd injured in the state championship high school football game—throbbed with pain as he held on for hours. "I just hugged that tree as hard as I could, waiting for the storm to blow past," he said. "It took forever. My shoulder was hurting so bad, I didn't know if I could hold on. But I knew if I let go, I'd get killed."

By evening the storm had passed, but a scene of utter devastation and horror surrounded them. Virtually every building had been flattened or blown away, leaving tens of thousands of people homeless and dozens dead from drowning or being hit by flying objects or falling trees.

"You couldn't get down to the city from there," said Greg. "All the roads were either washed out or blocked by fallen trees. It was awful. I didn't even think about leaving at that point. Everyone really needed help."

Greg spent weeks helping people rebuild after the storm. It was a trying time for everyone. The people there had always been poor, but they lived well for their means. Now they had nothing; the storm had destroyed everything they owned. Still, it was amazing how quickly they bounced back. Virtually right after the storm, people were gathering up pieces of their devastated homes—some materials had been carried more than 200 yards away—and trying to find their missing livestock: chickens, ducks, geese, and goats. The next morning, the sound of people hammering nails and sawing boards with handsaws rang out all around the village. Their determination was impressive and inspiring.

Finally, after staying in the village for several more weeks, Greg hiked back to Kingston to see about getting back home. It was tough to leave. He loved all the people in the village, and a lot of tears were shed as Greg said goodbye to Winston and all the new friends he'd met there. He made his way alone to the American Embassy and told them what had happened. They were very helpful and made arrangements to get him a new passport and a plane ticket to Miami, where his Uncle Donny could meet him at the airport. He had spent more than three months in Jamaica, but it seemed like years to Greg.

Living in the mountains, it had been too difficult to get down to the shore, so Greg hadn't been able to fish the entire time he was there. He hated to leave Jamaica without catching a single fish, so he went to the harbor to have a look around. There he met a couple of fishing guides who generously told him the location of an excellent place to fish nearby and even loaned him a rod and reel, despite the fact that he had no money to pay them. That afternoon as he was casting from the dock, reeling in again and again, a six-foot-long barracuda hammered his bait and took off, bending the rod double, the reel screaming as Greg fought to prevent its escape. He was back in the saddle again.

INTO THE WEST

Greg lay sprawled on the sidewalk in the glaring winter sun, his mind still shrouded in a fog as he struggled to regain consciousness. A policeman knelt over him, holding his hat above Greg to block the sunlight from his face. In great pain and feeling disoriented, as though returning from a long, dark journey, Greg felt the hot, wet blood on his face and could taste it in his mouth. Slowly it started coming back to him: climbing into his Jeep that morning; heading to the gym for a workout; passing a place he knew so well, the site of old Mr. Corey's trout farm. He thought about it even as he lay bleeding from multiple gashes and abrasions. But Corey's was long gone. Although the ponds still remained, the building had been replaced by an office complex that housed a medical insurance company. Yes, he remembered it now: he was driving through the intersection in front of Corey's; a van slammed into him broadside, flipping the Jeep, throwing him out—and he was flying through the air . . . until his face smashed against the pavement . . . and everything went dark.

Now the policeman was talking to him, asking him if he was okay. Greg recognized him—they had gone to high school together. "Don't worry, an ambulance is coming," the policeman said, then told Greg about the other driver, a security guard at the insurance company who had been driving one of their vans. He was now passed out in the driver's seat and he reeked of alcohol; he didn't even have a driver's license. Greg grimaced with pain when he tried to nod.

A distant siren became louder and louder until an ambulance pulled up right beside him. The EMTs jumped out and started working on him: checking his vital signs, putting a brace on his neck, hoisting him onto a stretcher, loading him into the ambulance, and finally rushing him to the hospital with the siren screaming. He was badly injured, with a smashed face, a concussion, and a broken nose. A big chunk of his scalp had been ripped out, he had a severe gash in his leg, and one of his fingers had nearly been torn off.

Greg closed his eyes and sighed as the emergency room nurses started an IV drip with a sedative and a painkiller. *One more time in the hospital,* he thought. *One more close call. Now what?* He'd be stuck in his parents' condo again, this time without a car; trapped there with his father in the basement, constantly begging Greg to kill him, his mother nagging at him, and no way to escape. But he didn't want to think about it now. He let the warm glow of the pain medication settle over him, carrying him away like a tidal drift, rocking him gently as he fell into a deep slumber.

When Greg was released from the hospital, he set out trying to line up an attorney and begin the process of mounting a lawsuit against the medical insurance company whose driver had nearly killed him. It seemed to Greg the case should be a slam dunk for anyone who wanted to take it, and the lawyer he approached, named Frank, agreed and set to work on it.

Of course, lawsuits always take months, and in the meantime Greg had to sit at his parents' condo with no money and no job prospects. His only transportation after his Jeep got totaled was an old dirt bike that wasn't even street legal. The bike's motor was extremely loud, and whenever he fired it up, the neighbors in the condo complex would call the police and complain, so he had to take off quickly and keep to the back roads.

He started riding out to some of the nearby farms, hoping to get a job. They didn't need anyone at any of the places he had worked previously, but one day he stopped at a local fruit orchard and talked to David Henry, the ninety-year-old owner, who quickly hired him. Greg felt right at home there, working alongside two crews of Jamaicans. The orchard grew mostly apples but also peaches, plums, nectarines, and blueberries. It was all of the finest quality, and it wasn't for local sale—all of the fruit was shipped overseas to the Netherlands and other lucrative European markets.

Old-man Henry was a character: tough, hardworking, and stoic. Once while Greg was working there, Mr. Henry had to go into the hospital for a couple of weeks to have open-heart surgery. On the very day he got back, with the stitches still in place where the surgeons had cracked open his chest, he was driving around on his tractor, working as hard as anyone.

As soon as Greg got to work each day, he would ride around with Mr. Henry in the company pickup truck, going up and down the orchard rows. A rifle lay on the dashboard. "He was a tough old bastard," said Greg. "He used to take me with him every morning when he went to hunt deer. He would shoot them with a rifle right out of the truck." Of course, this would be against the law if they were sport hunting, but Mr. Henry had a depredation permit, which allowed him to kill deer and other animals that were damaging his crops. Whenever they got a deer, Greg would help him load it into the back of the truck and take it to the Jamaicans, who would cook it up into a rich curry for everyone. "Working at the orchard was one of the healthiest times in my life— eating great Jamaican cooking and the homegrown fruit and vegetables we grew there."

Greg had to ride his dirt bike two miles to work each morning, but his neighbors were onto him and would call the police as soon as he fired it up. One day the cops red-lighted him, and he took off, reaching speeds of more than ninety miles an hour on the tiny back roads. He ducked into the farm, hid his dirt bike in a shed, put on a hardhat to help conceal his identity, jumped onto a tractor, and started driving it through the orchard, acting as though he had been there all morning. It worked—the cops pulled their prowl car into the farm and looked around for a while, but they didn't even glance twice at him.

Mr. Henry, who had seen the cops chasing Greg that day, mentioned that he had a car stored on the property that he would be happy to sell him. He walked over to the barn, slid the huge door open, and flipped on a light switch. Greg was stunned to see an immaculate blue 1977 Ford LTD, looking like it had just rolled off the assembly line. He opened the door and gazed inside at the plush seats and pristine dashboard, with an odometer that showed less than 40,000 miles. Mr. Henry had driven it in there years earlier, when it was only a couple years old, and never taken it out again. Mr. Henry said he would just deduct $100 a month from Greg's paycheck until the car was paid for.

Greg was a hard worker and within a month was put in charge of one of the crews of Jamaican laborers. It was a dream job for him. With his "management" position at the orchard, Greg was provided with an old house to live in. Although he was only paid $650 a month, free rent and utilities and much of his daily food were part of the deal. But best of all, he didn't ever have to go home. For months, his parents didn't even know where he was.

It was a good time for Greg. He had everything he needed. He started fishing with his old friends the Carlsons again, cruising all over Long Island Sound in their fishing boat, catching more striped bass than ever.

Meanwhile, the lawsuit slowly progressed. It took nearly a year for the case to be resolved, but at the end of the process Greg got a whopping settlement from the insurance company.

"I went from nothing to having a quarter of a million dollars," said Greg. He immediately paid Mr. Henry cash for what he still owed on the Ford LTD, counting out a stack of hundred-dollar bills on his kitchen table. He also went shopping for a brand-new Jeep to replace the one that had been destroyed in the accident.

"I bought myself this big, bad-ass Jeep CJ-7, California style," said Greg. "It was right off the cover of *4-Wheel Drive* magazine. I paid cash for it. And I bought all new clothes."

Several of his friends at the University of Rhode Island were about to graduate, so he drove there to attend the commencement ceremony and the parties that would follow. It had only been two years since he dropped out of URI after losing his athletic scholarship, but he showed up looking every inch the distinguished alum.

"My friends were like, 'What have you been up to?' 'Oh, just living the dream,'" said Greg.

He was an instant hit with his old classmates and went partying with them on the beach at Narragansett. Everyone wanted to know what he was doing, and he said he planned to head out across the country, fishing, partying, seeing all the sights, and having a great time. This idea had actually only occurred to him a few weeks earlier, when his old babysitter, Alice, who had taken care of him as a young child when they lived in Hamden, returned to Connecticut with her fiancé to get married there. Alice came from a troubled family, and Herb Myerson had helped her escape that situation. He'd encouraged her to join the Air Force, and soon afterwards she had moved to Nevada. She called Greg and asked if he would give her away at her wedding, because she didn't have a father, and he agreed.

"The guy she was marrying, Danny, was a poker player at a casino and had lived his whole life in Reno, which is a desert," said Greg. "I remember when they landed here, I heard him telling his friend on the phone, 'Oh, my God, It's like a jungle here. You can't even see into the woods. It's hot and humid.' He'd never left Nevada before."

But Greg took a liking to Danny—they were both avid snow skiers. The couple stayed with Greg in his house at the Henry farm the entire time they were in Connecticut. After the wedding, they told him if he ever wanted to go out West, he'd always have a place to stay at their home.

So now, as he hung around with his friends who were graduating from URI, he decided he would take Alice and Danny up on their offer and head to Nevada. At the graduation party, Greg ran into his friend Butch from Portland, Maine, who had been a defensive lineman on the university's football team with Greg until he broke his neck in a game, ending his athletic career. He listened with great interest to Greg's plans for a cross-country driving adventure.

"Oh man, I'd love to come," he said.

"Well, why don't you?" asked Greg.

"I don't have enough money."

"I've got plenty for both of us. I'll cover everything."

At that point, Greg was still living at the Henry farm, but he wasn't working there anymore, so they were getting ready to toss him out of the house.

"I had all this money, so I just fished and partied all night and played golf during the day. I thought about getting a boat, but I knew I would be leaving soon. And the Carlsons were still letting me use their boat whenever I wanted."

Butch finally called Greg back and said he definitely wanted to go. The next day Greg picked him up in the big blue LTD, a great cross-country cruiser. He left his new Jeep behind with some friends.

On their first day, they drove to Atlantic City, New Jersey, the epicenter of East Coast gambling. Greg was determined to do everything as over-the-top as possible on their journey, so he stopped en route and bought them both great new suits. At the hotel, Greg asked for the penthouse suite and put all of their cash and travelers' checks in the hotel safe.

Greg started making wild bets on the roulette wheel the minute he got to the casino, laying down $100 or more at a pop. He had a vision that this would be the journey to end all journeys, a blur of wild partying from one end of the country to the other. They would party down until all the money was gone, and then figure out what to do to keep going. Why worry? Butch looked a lot like Elvis Presley, so they joked that he could do some Elvis impersonations to make money. But as it turned out, Greg couldn't lose at the roulette table. He hit . . . and hit . . . and hit. It was crazy. They walked out of the casino with an additional $20,000.

Next they stopped to see some friends in Virginia Beach for a few days, and then headed to Atlanta to visit some of their former classmates from URI. While they were there, Greg met a beautiful woman from North Carolina who was living in Atlanta, and he ended up moving in with her for three weeks. Butch was completely at his mercy —Greg had the car and all of the money—and called him every day, asking, "What's the deal? Are we going?" They'd been gone for nearly a month, ostensibly to drive out West, and they were still stuck on the East Coast. But eventually the day came when Greg said, "All right, let's go." They loaded up the LTD and pointed it westward. As they peeled away, Greg asked, "So, where you wanna go?" This would become an almost daily mantra for Greg.

In some ways, they were like the Odd Couple. Butch always had everything figured out for the trip, including a list of places he wanted to visit and things he wanted to do as they traveled across America. Greg could care less about any of that. Butch would pull out the map and start planning the day's journey as Greg drove.

"Let's go to the Jack Daniel's distillery," said Butch. So they headed to Lynchburg, Tennessee. Next, "I want to see Graceland." So they drove across the state to Memphis and dropped in at Elvis Presley's house. Then it was on to Oklahoma City, where they hung out for a while before driving down into Texas, taking Highway 40 to Amarillo. It was all a wild, impressionistic blur as they streaked down the road, stopping at various sites Butch had marked along the way.

They left Texas and drove to New Mexico so Greg could go fishing on the famed San Juan River, one of the top trophy trout rivers in the country. Greg loved it and caught several huge trout, but Butch was eager to see Colorado, so they left a few days later. They met two women there and wound up staying at their apartment for a couple of weeks while Greg fly fished. But one day they got the itch to move and disappeared without another word, heading west once more — to Salt Lake City, to the rock formations, to Moab, to Monument Valley. They hiked. They went mountain biking. Greg went fishing.

On the open terrain of Utah and Nevada, Greg opened up the throttle of the LTD, rocketing down the highway at blistering speeds, sometimes driving 130 mph for an hour or more at a time. Butch would scour the distant vista with his 10x binoculars, trying to spot any cops who might be lurking up ahead with a speed trap. The journey became a blur of pastel colors — sand, desert rocks, and pale blue sky — as panicked jackrabbits raced back and forth across the hot tarmac to avoid being hit.

Greg and Butch finally arrived in Reno. Danny and Alice were great hosts and gave each of them their own spacious room in their house for as long as they wanted to visit. Danny had a speedboat, and they would all drive to Pyramid Lake to water-ski at least once a week. Greg went fly fishing there for native Lahontan cutthroat trout, the state fish of Nevada. He also hiked into the Sierra Nevada Mountains to fish the remote streams and tiny lakes of the high country. The trout there were small but vividly colored, and he enjoyed catching and releasing them. Once, a bear surprised him as he stood beside a creek, casting dry flies at trout; it roared loudly at Greg to make him leave. As soon as he turned to walk away, the bear splashed into the water, trying to catch some trout.

Greg and Butch eventually started painting houses to earn some money. "We met this guy who was a drunk, but he had a spray-gun machine to paint houses, and he was good at it," said Greg. "But I noticed right away, the people out there are not hustlers like we are in the East. I started landing all these jobs painting houses, and all he wanted for spray-painting them was thirty bucks and a case of beer." Greg and

Butch did all the prep work and paid for materials, but they charged hundreds of dollars to paint each house. "We were making all kinds of money." The job finally fizzled out when the painter became ill, so they were left looking for something else to do to keep busy.

Greg connected with two old Lyman Hall friends, Bill and Ralph, who had played on the football team with him. The two had been sharing an apartment in San Francisco, but Ralph was currently working in Reno. Ralph knew a woman who had gone to Lyman Hall with them and was now leasing a condominium on the shore of Lake Tahoe, so they went to visit her. She told them she couldn't afford the place anymore, but they were welcome to take over the lease if they wanted to live there together. It was a beautiful but expensive condo in picturesque Incline Village. Greg, Ralph, Bill, and Butch decided to move into it together and split the cost.

"I got a job as a bouncer at a nightclub in Tahoe," said Greg. "It was great. People were slipping me hundred-dollar bills. I let anyone in — sometimes parties of a couple hundred people from Las Vegas or Los Angeles. I really didn't care who came in. I met a lot of people."

Greg would occasionally get invited to some big houses along the lake that had their own casinos inside, complete with roulette and blackjack tables. Some nights Greg would act as the bank, fronting all the gambling money and taking a major cut of the action.

"I'd put up $10,000 and walk out with $20,000," said Greg. "I was loving it there."

Greg called up his friends Brad and Verne in Connecticut and told them what a great time he was having and that he had a condo on Lake Tahoe where they were welcome to stay.

"I'm living it up here," he said. "Things are really great."

"We're coming!" they told him. So they drove Greg's Jeep all the way to Lake Tahoe and moved in with him.

"It was really crazy, just like *Animal House*," said Greg. "We spent the summer there, and it was the greatest thing. I would go driving along in my Jeep through the desert with the top down, with the stereo blasting the Eagles' 'Hotel California.' I was hanging out with UCLA students on the beaches at Lake Tahoe and meeting all kinds of skiers and famous people at the club. But my money was starting to dwindle away. I was just burning through it."

Of course, Greg was still going fishing every day, but now he and his friends really needed the fish to eat. "By then, we were all eating these chicken pot pies every day, two for seventy-five cents at the 7-Eleven," said Greg. He decided to try a new spot on Lake Tahoe that looked promising. Parking his Jeep, he hiked down to the beach and started rigging up his fly rod. Then he happened to look at some of the nearby sunbathers and noticed they were naked. It was a nude beach. "So I said, 'What the hell?' and stripped off all my clothes." He stood on a rock near the shore, casting flies, and caught the biggest trout of his en-tire western journey—an eight-pounder. "I had to carry this huge fish back across the rocks and along the beach with no clothes on, stepping over naked sunbathers." The trout fed Greg and his friends for days.

But it felt like their western adventure was nearing the end. It wasn't just the lack of money—a sense of weariness was setting in with all of them. Greg was still partying as hard as ever, abusing alcohol and drugs and getting into fights whenever anyone challenged him. "The party-ing and all of the shit that was going on," said Greg. "We were starting to get in trouble, and the cops had their eyes on me."

A short time later, Butch said he'd had enough and bought a plane ticket back home to Maine. Not long after that, Greg began gazing longingly eastward and thinking about home. Before leaving Connect-icut, he'd had the foresight to stash $5,000 in cash in the garage at his parents' condo, so he wasn't broke. And he'd recently gotten a phone call from his old boss, Joe, at the electrical company in New Haven where he'd worked summers during college. Joe had lost one of his workers and needed to replace him. He knew Greg would be the per-fect man for the job, because he was hardworking and knew the Yale campus so well, where the company had its most important projects. Joe told him if he came back from Lake Tahoe, he'd give him the job and also get him into the International Brotherhood of Electrical Engineers apprenticeship program, so he could become a union electrician.

That was all it took. Greg loaded up all his belongings and began the long journey homeward.

THE DEERSLAYER

With the money Greg was earning from his work in the electricians'
union, he started going on trout-fishing trips with his friend Bear Judkins from college. Greg had introduced Bear to fly fishing, and now he
couldn't get enough. They traveled together to rivers and streams all
around the Northeast and also sometimes headed west to the famed San
Juan River in New Mexico and to Colorado. They often camped along
the Kennebec River in Maine. On one of their trips driving through
Vermont, they found a cabin along the White River near Bethel and
decided to split the cost and buy it together. In addition to being avid
anglers, they both loved snow skiing, so the place was perfect—right
on a river and close to Killington Ski Resort.

"We became regulars at Killington and would ski about a hundred
days a year there," said Greg. "Whenever my union jobs finished and
I got laid off, I would go up there and work for the steak house at Killington, beating up people who were out of control. Killington owned
it, so I had a free season ski pass. So it was skiing in the winter and fly
fishing in spring."

But in autumn, as the chill of the changing seasons settled over the land, Greg's mind always turned to hunting. He had seen a great buck several times in early fall, always in the same area—a small meadow in the woods along Highway 107, at the edge of the Green Mountains, just a couple of miles from his cabin. It was big, easily topping 200 pounds, with the best rack he'd ever seen on a whitetail. He couldn't help thinking about it as deer season approached. This was his buck, and his alone. He knew he would be there waiting at the edge of the meadow as dawn approached on opening day.

Several friends stayed at his cabin the night before and planned to go deer hunting nearby, but Greg didn't tell them about his buck. He got up before anyone else and stood drinking a cup of hot coffee, staring out the window as the first snow of the season fell in the darkness, accumulating quickly on the ground outside. Everything was ready: his rifle was clean and oiled; his scope sighted-in. As his friends slumbered, he slung the rifle over his shoulder and stepped outside.

It was a black, moonless night, and he hadn't brought a flashlight, but he knew the way by heart. He hiked a couple of miles down the small two-lane highway, then turned at the place where the forest opened into the small meadow the buck frequented. Snow was falling heavily, thick and fluffy, as Greg made his way carefully into the woods. He sat quietly at the edge of the meadow, waiting as the first rays of daylight began illuminating the forest. All of his senses were tuned perfectly to his surroundings—his ears, his eyes, his very spirit. The woods seemed to pulsate like a single organism, living and breathing around him and within him. He felt a complete awareness of everything: the ground, the trees, the wind sighing through the treetops, and the falling snow. He shuddered for an instant and turned his collar against the cold.

A faint rustle broke the silence ahead of him in the woods; then everything was still again. Greg made his way swiftly to where the sound had come from, but there was nothing—except a bare patch on the ground where the buck had made a scrape. (In rutting season, bucks will scrape the ground and urinate there to leave a scent and announce their presence.) Greg knew it was fresh; the snow had not even begun to cover it yet. He saw the deer tracks leading away, up the steep mountainside. As the early morning began to brighten, he peered upward along the side of the mountain, his eyes tracing the buck's most likely path. He did a double take as he finally spotted the deer, standing on a promontory, looking back down. The buck obviously knew he was being followed and was trying to see who or what was after him.

Greg and the buck were engaged in an ancient dance—predator and prey—and they both knew it. Greg's heart was racing as he knelt in the snow and carefully raised the rifle to his eye. But it was no good: the eyepiece of the scope had filled with snow. He cursed his stupidity for letting this happen and quickly cleaned out the snow with the thumb of his glove. Raising the scope to his eye again, he saw that it was fogged, but by pressing his face hard against the eyepiece, he could make out the shape of the deer. Greg tried to relax, inhaling deeply, then slowly released his breath as he squeezed the trigger.

The rifle's recoil slammed the scope into Greg's face, knocking him to the ground. He lay there stunned and barely conscious for several minutes. As he came to, his face felt burning hot and wet, and he realized it was covered with blood. He slipped the glove from his right hand and felt his face. Having broken his nose several times before, both playing football and in fights, he recognized the feeling at once. He grabbed a handful of snow and held it against his face until the flow of blood slowed and then stopped. Then he raised himself to his knees.

Where was the deer? He knew the buck had lurched just before the rifle fired. Had Greg missed the shot? He had no idea. He didn't even know how long he'd lain there before coming to. He got up quickly and hiked to the spot where the buck had stood when he fired. The buck's tracks were there, but there was no sign of it now, and no trace of any blood. It must have been a clean miss. But he saw its tracks in the fresh snow, going higher and higher up the mountainside, and he felt his blood rising inside him. He raced after the buck, going ever higher and deeper into the Green Mountains, moving down through deep ravines and up again to lofty ridgelines. Hours went by—he had no idea how many. Single-minded in his pursuit, Greg felt no pain, hunger, or thirst. He was oblivious to the cold and didn't even consider his own survival. His sole focus was on killing the buck. At that moment, it was his only reason to exist.

Greg didn't see the buck for hours, but he never lost sight of its tracks. Occasionally he would come to a spot where the buck had paused at a vantage point to peer back down the mountain, to see if Greg was still following. No doubt it felt the psychological pressure of being pursued by a relentless predator. For the buck, losing this battle would mean the end of its life—but Greg, too, had his life on the line. He was mentally incapable of giving up this chase, even though all common sense argued strongly against continuing. He would get that deer or die trying.

Shortly before dusk, Greg pulled himself over a ridgetop, and there was the buck, standing right before him, less than fifty yards away. He was taken aback for an instant by the sight of it and hesitated. The two of them were exhausted. Greg sensed the buck had given up, worn down by his unrelenting pursuit. The end was almost anticlimactic: Greg raised his rifle, took careful aim, and fired; the buck dropped without even taking a step.

But now what? It was getting dark and, in his obsession to kill the buck, Greg hadn't paid attention to where he was going all day. He had not stopped once to eat or drink or rest. He was hungry, exhausted, and dehydrated. He had spent all day pursuing the buck, and now that he had killed it, the deer had become a huge liability for him. It was much too big to haul out that night, and he didn't have any idea where he was. He knew if he left it out overnight, animals would find it and feed on it, and everything would have been a waste—all the effort and brutal hardships of this day. But worse, this magnificent animal would have been killed for nothing, and that knowledge gnawed at Greg.

He looked at the trees around him. *Maybe I can haul the buck into one of them,* he thought. He took out his hunting knife and quickly made a vertical slit from the anus to the sternum of the deer, then pulled its guts out onto the snow-covered ground, where they lay steaming in the cold. But the buck still weighed well over 150 pounds. Greg grabbed it in a headlock, dragged it to the nearest tree, and began climbing up the lowest branches, moving upward one step at a time, clinging to the deer. By the time he'd climbed five feet up the tree, he was panting and nauseated from the effort. And he was covered in blood—both his own from when the scope had struck his face and the deer's from its open gut cavity.

But he was determined to keep climbing, even as the deer's antlers poked him in the face, drawing more blood as he held the buck tightly in a headlock. The effort was excruciating. When he had the buck seven feet above the ground, he stopped. *At least it's out of the reach of coyotes,* he thought. After weaving some branches between the deer's legs to keep it from falling, he jumped back down to the ground and tried to catch his breath.

What was he to do now? The snow lay knee-deep in places, and the day had turned bitterly cold as soon as the sun went down. He had sweated profusely as he hauled the deer into the tree, and now he felt chilled. And he hadn't brought anything to eat. *Where the hell am I?* he thought. *How the fuck am I going to get out of here?* Moonlight reflecting off the snow provided some illumination, but there was nothing to follow. *Just head downhill, I guess, and hope I run into a trail,* he thought.

When he finally stumbled upon an old logging trail, he followed it downward, hoping to find a way off the mountain. By this time, he was shivering uncontrollably. His clothing wasn't warm enough to spend the night hunkered in the bushes, waiting for morning. He had to keep moving. But was he just going deeper and deeper into the mountains? The snowfall had covered his tracks so he had no way of knowing. He'd just have to stay on the trail and hope it led somewhere. No one would be out searching for him here—no one knew where he was. He hadn't even told his friends which direction he was heading when he left the cabin, because he didn't want them to know about the big buck.

Greg sighed deeply as he looked up at the snow falling heavily down on him. He couldn't quit now; he had to keep going, all night long if necessary, if he was to have any chance of surviving until morning. Slinging the rifle over his shoulder, he made his way along the logging road, which first took him uphill again. When he finally crested the ridge, he thought he saw a tiny glimmer of light far below, but after taking a few steps, he couldn't make it out anymore. He began scrambling desperately in the direction he thought he had seen it, following the trail downward as it wound through the forest. And suddenly, there it was, emerging in a clearing up ahead—a tiny shack, perhaps only twelve by fifteen feet, with a camp lantern glowing inside. Greg pounded on the door.

"Who the hell is it?" came a gruff voice from inside, and Greg heard the click of a pistol being cocked. Then the door opened.

With his broken nose and the blood covering him nearly from head to foot, Greg must have looked like Leonardo DiCaprio's character from *The Revenant* after being mauled by the bear. The man instantly uncocked his gun and put it down.

"Jesus! What the hell happened to you?" he said. "Come on inside and get warmed up." Although he had a small camp heater blazing in the corner, it was barely any warmer inside than out, but at least it was out of the wind and snow. The man was older—in his early sixties and grizzled. He smiled at Greg and shook his head. "It's damn lucky you found this place," he said. "I built it four or five years ago and use it for deer hunting."

Greg began shivering uncontrollably as he sat down inside. "Let me get you some coffee," the man said. He reached behind him, struck a match, and lit the burner on a battered Coleman stove perched on a shelf beside him. He had a percolator half full of old coffee, and he set it on the burner to reheat.

"Thanks," said Greg as the man handed him a cup of the bitter black brew. "I was up here hunting deer, and I had a little accident."

"It sure looks like it," the man said, laughing. Greg told him about getting slammed in the face by the scope when he fired a shot. "You know, I never shot that rifle before. I bought it at a tag sale a couple weeks ago. The scope got all fogged up from the snow, so I had to hold it too close to my eye." Greg didn't tell him about killing the big buck and hanging it up in a tree. He didn't know this guy and was worried he might go back and take his deer. But it must have been obvious Greg was covered with more than just his own blood.

"Where you from, anyway?" the man asked, and Greg described the location of his cabin. "Holy shit! We're ten miles from there! You walked all that way in the snow?"

Greg nodded. He was so cramped and dehydrated, he could barely walk another step. The man offered to drive him home, and they trudged outside to his pickup truck. After quickly cleaning the snow off the windshield, he fired up the truck and drove down the mountain.

Greg's friends were shocked when he walked in the door. Of course, they hadn't called anyone to go searching for him. They'd all given up on deer hunting early in the day and come back to the cabin to start the drinking and partying they had really come there for. Greg told them he'd killed the biggest deer he'd ever seen after chasing it ten miles into the mountains. Their attitude was, "Yeah, right. Sure!"

"Whatever," he said. He walked back to his room and fell down across his bed, dropping into a deep slumber without even changing his clothes or washing the blood from his face. He slept for fourteen hours.

The next day, Greg went back to get the deer, but he couldn't find the place. All of his tracks had been covered by fresh snowfall and blowing drifts during the night. He spent all day hiking, searching for the buck, determined to find it. The weather was cold so the meat should be in good shape for days, he reasoned. It became an overpowering obsession.

"I looked for that buck for months," Greg told me. "But it wasn't until the next spring that I finally found it. The only thing left was the spinal cord and head, with a massive rack on it. Something had pulled it down, and it was picked clean. It was just like in *The Old Man and the Sea,* when the man finally caught the big fish, and the sharks ate it. It was all my fault. I just went too far."

AFTER THE STORM

After graduating from Yale, Dave Myerson enlisted as an officer in the Marine Corps and was in the vanguard of Operation Desert Storm in 1990, America's first Gulf War. Although Greg never let on to his friends and family, this was an incredibly stressful time for him. He was so worried that Dave might get seriously injured or killed that he thought about it all the time, whether he was working, fishing, or lying in bed, struggling to get to sleep. And then, six months after the war began, it was over, and the troops started coming home.

Greg finally saw his brother on the day before Easter 1991, and went out to celebrate his return with several of Dave's Yale friends. All of them knew Greg well. When he was still in high school, he had come to visit Dave and his friends often, and they had taken him under their wing. He would stay with them in their huge penthouse apartment on Chapel Street in New Haven whenever he was at odds with his mother about his wild behavior. They used to call him "the Townie" and let him help them with the pranks and mischief they pulled against other frat houses and colleges. They even helped him establish a fake identity as a Yale student so he could meet coeds.

"They told me what to tell the freshman girls and gave me a whole Yale résumé to memorize, with classes I was supposedly taking and the professors' names," said Greg. "I had many Yale girlfriends thanks to them."

Greg had also helped them out on their graduation day. He had gotten dressed up and gone to Yale with his family. Everyone was there —his parents, aunts and uncles, and friends—all waiting to see Dave receive his diploma. But Dave didn't show up. Herb finally pulled Greg aside and said, "Go find your brother." So he ran down Chapel Street to their apartment and, since he had his own key, went right inside. The graduation was already in progress.

"So I had to lead these six Yale students down the street, all disheveled and fucked up, to their graduation," said Greg. "And they were drinking a bottle of gin as they were walking there. I was laughing and loving it, because I wanted to see the reaction of their families when they showed up. These guys were crazy."

Dave's fraternity friends were a lot different now, all married and well-off looking—not the same wild bunch they had been just a couple of years earlier. But they decided to go out on the town and get smashed for old times' sake, and they took Greg with them.

They all got staggering drunk, especially Greg, who felt such an intense sense of relief that his brother had returned unharmed from the war, he kept breaking down and crying most of the night. But on the way home he turned violent. Three people rode in the front seat of the car, so Greg and Dave had the back seat to themselves. Suddenly, without warning, they were brawling with each other, just as they'd done so many times as kids and later in high school, shouting and throwing punches. When they got to the place where Greg was living, he and Dave spilled out of the car together. Greg landed a final crushing blow, hitting Dave in the eye, almost knocking him unconscious. His friends got Dave back in the car and quickly drove him to his parents' condominium.

To Greg—and perhaps Dave as well—this was no big deal. Greg had obviously been dealing with a lot of stress worrying about his brother, and ironically, he ended up relieving the stress by pummeling him. (Perhaps only Dave was capable of understanding that.) The next morning when he arrived for Easter dinner at his parents' condo, he didn't even suspect anything might be wrong.

"Hey, Mom, happy Easter!" he said. His mother glared at him and turned away, furious, and his aunts wouldn't even look at him.

"So what's up?" he asked.

Diane turned and shouted in his face: "Your brother fights in a war for six months and comes out without a scratch. And then you almost beat him to death? What kind of animal are you?"

"What are you talking about?" he said.

"You make me sick!" She turned away in disgust and left the room.

Greg walked downstairs to his father's living quarters. Herb, no longer able to get up by himself, was sitting in the special chair that could lift him to standing position. Dave lay passed out on the downstairs couch, his black eye showing. Herb stared up at Greg as he walked past but didn't say anything. Greg went to the couch and stood over Dave, looking down at his bruised face. He started poking him in the ribs to wake him up. As Dave opened his eyes, Greg loomed above him, his fist cocked, ready to punch him in the face. Dave just smiled, closed his eyes, and rolled over.

"He knew I was just fucking around, you know," said Greg. "That's the way we were; we were brutal. We were both linebackers, for Christ's sake. My brother used to say these wrestling terms or names of famous wrestlers, and that would set us off. We'd be in the middle of a family function or something, and all of a sudden he'd say something like, 'The Anvil of Death will get you.' And he'd jump on me or pile-drive me into the ground, or break the table or something, sending food flying everywhere. My mother would be screaming," he said, laughing. "It was really fucked up."

WOUNDED TIGER

Maybe it was inevitable that Brian Jackson and Greg would tangle someday. Their history just went back too far—back to the days in grade school when Brian would torment and torture his younger brother Scott and Greg, often slapping them around and taking their money. Tall and powerfully built, he had been a bully his entire life, and he was fearless, instantly ready to fight with anyone, no matter how the odds might be stacked against him. As bad as he was to Scott and Greg, Brian was ten times worse to other people. His ferocity was legendary around town. One night when Greg was sixteen, he and some friends went to East Rock Park—a popular hangout overlooking Yale and all of New Haven, where people went to drink and party—when he saw Brian get in a fight with another man even larger than him. The guy pulled a knife and slashed Brian's abdomen wide open, but it only made Brian more dangerous, like a wounded tiger, enraged and terrifying in the intensity of his attack. With blood streaming from his wound, he pummeled the man with his fist again and again and again, turning his face to pulp, while holding his guts in with his other hand.

Later, it took more than 175 stitches in the emergency room to close the knife cut in his abdomen.

Brian spent a good part of his life behind bars. It didn't have to be that way—he was a truly talented athlete, the best baseball player Greg had ever known. He played in the Babe Ruth League with Dave when they were growing up and was a fabulous hitter. Everyone said he could easily have played in the major leagues. And he was handsome. Standing six foot four and weighing 250 pounds, he bore a striking resemblance to the actor Matt Dillon. Diane Myerson had always taken an interest in Brian and encouraged him to strive to be something better, just as she had pushed Dave and Greg. But it was no good. Brian seemed to have a chip on his shoulder against the whole world. He went through life perpetually in trouble, and brought trouble to everyone around him. As a teen, he was always getting arrested and sent to juvenile detention, and when he reached adulthood, he was in and out of prison. He would get busted for burglary, drugs, fighting, robbery, muggings—whatever. There was nothing he wouldn't do.

Growing up, Greg had tried to avoid crossing Brian, but by his early twenties something had changed. He'd become tougher and harder. Maybe it was the frustrations in his life: watching his father slowly waste away; being nagged by his mother; losing his scholarship at the University of Rhode Island; or the effects from years of playing football in high school and college. And he'd been in several particularly brutal fights, like the brawl at the frat house in college. He felt immune to pain and was absolutely convinced he was much tougher and more dangerous than anyone else.

But still—Brian Jackson. You fight him, you fight to the death—his or yours. Everyone knew that. There was no halfway in dealing with him.

It all came to a head one night when Greg's brother was on leave from the Marines and the two went out together. They had gone fishing earlier in the day and were sitting at a local bar when Brian walked in. They were surprised to see him—he'd been in prison for the past couple of years. He spotted Greg and Dave right away and walked up to them.

"Hey, Greg, where the fuck's that money you owe me?" he asked.

Greg and Dave ignored him. Brian ordered a double Scotch and flirted briefly with the barmaid.

"Let's get out of here," said Dave, and laid some money on the bar to pay for their drinks. They walked out to the parking lot, but Brian followed them outside.

"Don't be fucking with me, man. I want my money," said Brian.

Greg wasn't having any part of it. Brian was always hitting Greg and other people up for money like that, claiming they owed him. It had been that way as long as Greg could remember, and he'd had it.

"Fuck you!" said Greg. "I don't owe you shit."

Greg and Dave had driven separate vehicles to the bar, so Dave got in his car as Greg opened the door of his pickup truck and stepped inside. It was only a two-minute drive to Greg's apartment, just down the road in Morris Cove. But Brian opened the passenger door and climbed in beside Greg.

"Look, fucker, I want my money," he said.

A feeling of scary calm descended over Greg. He glared at Brian. "I tell you what," said Greg. "We'll straighten this out in a minute when I get to my place."

By the time Greg pulled into the parking lot at his apartment, Dave was there, as well as several other people from the bar. It was just after 2:00 a.m., and the bar had just closed. Greg got out and walked around to the other side of the truck where Brian stood waiting. Without warning, he slammed his fist into Brian's face with all his might, knocking out several teeth and sending him reeling backward ten feet, then crashing flat on the ground. Despite the crushing blow, Brian burst up instantly, lunging at Greg, who punched him again and threw him hard against the side of the truck. Brian spotted the bag of golf clubs in the bed of the pickup, grabbed one, and swung it hard at Greg's head, missing by a quarter of an inch with a great *whoosh* as Greg dodged. Brian swung the club wildly again and again, with all the speed and power of a major league batter, as Greg backed up, frantically trying to avoid being hit, which would probably have killed him.

Then Greg spun around with a roundhouse kick, his foot connecting hard with Brian's face, sending him sprawling to the ground again. Before he could get up, Greg grabbed him by the hair and lifted his head up, then punched him repeatedly in the face—*wham, wham, wham!* By this time the other people in the parking lot were trying to break up the fight.

"Look, Greg, someone's going to get killed here," Dave yelled. "It's not worth it."

"Get the fuck away from me!" shouted Greg as he punched his brother in the face. Then he took a couple of swings at other people. "Get the hell out of here!"

Dave was furious. "Shit, I'm out of here," he said. "I don't want to be here when this ends, Greg. I don't want any part of it." Dave and the others went back to their cars and drove away. Greg looked back at Brian, lying in a pool of blood on the asphalt, and figured the fight was all over. He left him and walked into his apartment. Greg's friend Verne was asleep on the couch in his living room and woke up as he walked inside. He saw the blood all over Greg.

"What the hell happened?" asked Verne.

"I just beat the living shit out of Brian Jackson," he said.

Bang! A loud smash echoed through the apartment as something slammed against the front door. Then *Bang!*—a few seconds later another. Greg peeked out the window and saw Brian throwing a huge cinder block at the door, trying to break it down. Greg walked to the back of his apartment, slipped quietly out the sliding glass door onto the deck, and then snuck around to the front. He watched as Brian picked up the cinder block again and hurled it against the door. Then Greg leapt out at him, striking him with a devastating blow against the side of his head. This time when Brian went down, Greg was on him, pounding him again and again and again until blood was splashing up all over Greg, and still he hit him until he was too exhausted to lift his arms.

And then the fire in Greg began slowly diminishing, and he saw for the first time the gravity of the situation—how still Brian lay. He noticed, with horror, that Brian wasn't breathing.

From that point on, it was like an out-of-body experience for Greg as he mechanically went through the motions of dragging Brian by his jacket out to his pickup truck, opening the tailgate, and struggling to lift his limp body into the bed of the truck. He knew at some level what he had to do. As a fisherman, he was acutely aware of the tides and knew it was now high tide. He could picture it all in his mind: the Tomlinson Road bridge, five minutes away, with tidal water now flooding under it, which would start to recede within an hour, sucking anything in the estuary out to Long Island Sound. There a body might go days or weeks before showing up, perhaps miles away—or it might even be swept out to the Atlantic, never to be seen again.

Greg pulled up and parked at the bridge a few minutes later. It was quiet, dark, and desolate there at three in the morning, with a chill in the air that sent a shudder through his body. He took a deep breath and tried to calm down. He could feel that this was a terrifying turning point in his life, and nothing would ever be the same again. He lit a cigarette and took a couple of deep drags, then tossed it away into the night. Stepping outside, he walked to the back of the truck—and suddenly Brian burst up from the truck bed and took a swing at Greg, like a ghastly nightmare brought to life. Horrified, Greg swung wildly and struck Brian in the head, knocking him out again.

Abruptly, Greg changed direction. He drove to the farmhouse where Brian's family lived and carried him up the stairs onto the front porch. He banged hard with his fist until the lights came on and Brian's parents opened the door. Greg dragged Brian inside and laid him down on the kitchen floor.

Brian's mother was in shock. "What happened?" she asked.

"We got into a fight."

"Who did you fight with?"

Greg looked away. "With each other." He walked out of the kitchen, went upstairs to Scott's room, and turned on the light. Scott awoke from a deep sleep, blinking in the harsh light. He looked up at Greg, who stood before him, covered in blood.

"I just had a fight with your brother," said Greg. He looked down at the floor. "I think he might die."

Scott grimaced for an instant, then said, "Good. It was bound to happen sometime. I'm sure he had it coming."

Greg went home and, without bothering to clean up, crashed on top of his bed. But the grim aftermath of his fight with Brian did not end that night. The next morning, Verne and another friend, Charlie, were loading up the boat and getting ready to go fishing. Greg's apartment was right on the water at Morris Cove, and Verne kept the boat they shared just on the other side of the seawall. Greg walked outside, shirtless, and stood on the seawall to talk to his friends and let them know he wouldn't be going fishing with them. Verne and Charlie were amazed when they saw him.

"What's that huge lump on your stomach?" asked Verne. "And look at your hand." Greg had a great bulge along the side of his abdomen, and his left hand was so ballooned up it looked like an inflated rubber glove. Greg shrugged. He knelt down and started washing his hand off in seawater.

"You better go see a doctor," said Verne.

"I just sat there smoking a cigarette, watching them," Greg told me. "I was a mess, blood all over me."

After his friends motored off in the boat, Greg took a shower and changed his clothes. He looked at his left hand again, and it had gotten even worse. He had deep gouges where Brian's broken teeth had cut into his flesh as he punched him, and it was seriously inflamed, with red lines running up his arm. He decided not to wait any longer and drove himself to the emergency room. The doctor who examined him asked him what had happened. He looked very concerned when Greg told him.

"If the infection spreads, you might lose your hand," said the doctor. He admitted Greg to the hospital immediately and said he would need an antibiotic IV drip round the clock. What the doctor didn't tell him was that the infection was so bad Greg might even lose his life. He had cellulitis, which can quickly progress to sepsis and move throughout a person's body, leading to death in a matter of days.

Fifteen minutes later, Greg was lying in a hospital bed with his swollen hand suspended above him. But Greg had another problem. His intake of drugs and alcohol was so great—he was putting away a liter of Jack Daniel's and a least a gram of cocaine every day—he was in deep withdrawal. His craving was so bad he took his IV stand and wheeled it to the elevator, went downstairs, and walked out on Congress Avenue in his hospital gown, hoping to get some drugs and alcohol from someone, anyone. His doctor was just about to walk into the hospital when he spotted him.

"What are you doing outside?" he asked. "You're not supposed to be here."

Greg told him honestly what he was up to, and the doctor took him back upstairs. He started feeling Greg's swollen liver, then arranged for some lab tests. Greg's liver was nearly the size of a football—three times larger than normal. The doctor added a sedative to the IV drip to help relieve the withdrawal symptoms.

Greg remained in the hospital room recovering from the infection for the next seventeen days. When he was released from the hospital, his uncle drove him to rehab—at the strong urging of his doctor and his family—but he had to stop by his apartment on the way to pick up some clothes. As he walked inside, two of his friends were there, snorting lines of cocaine laid out on top of his television.

"I didn't have any desire to party at all," said Greg. His uncle was outside in the driveway, waiting in his car for Greg. The two of them drove to the rehab facility where Greg would spend the next month.

Brian recovered from the fight and ended up going to prison for seven years a short time later. Greg couldn't help wondering what would happen when Brian was released. He had knocked out most of his teeth. He wondered what Brian would be thinking about while he was locked up. What if he spent his entire sentence remembering what Greg had done and planning his revenge? What if he was pumping iron every day, working to get in top shape, just living for the day when he could get out and kill him?

Greg went to see Brian a day or two after his release from prison. Brian was lying on a chaise lounge in his family's backyard, trying to soak up some sun. He was pale and huge, like some beached whale—nothing like the young stud he had been seven years earlier when Greg beat him nearly to death.

Greg walked up to him as he lay there. Brian looked up, raising his hand over his eyes to shade them from the bright morning sunlight. "What's up?" he asked.

"Well, I just want to say, if you want a piece of me, we should just get it over with right now," said Greg. "I don't want to spend the rest of my life looking over my shoulder."

"Naw, fuck that," said Brian. "I don't care about that anymore."

And that was the end of it. Why did Brian decide not to go at it with Greg again? Had he become mellow with age? Maybe. But far more likely, he recognized that Greg had become even more dangerous than him, and their next fight would be to the death—and perhaps it just wasn't worth it.

But Greg will never forget that night or how fortunate it was the way it all turned out. He still feels sick when he thinks back on that moment as he sat in his truck, about to dump Brian off the bridge. "If I had thrown him off that bridge, my whole life would have changed instantly," he said. "I would have been a murderer. You just don't come back from something like that."

ROCK BOTTOM

How do you know when you've hit rock bottom? What does it take to finally snap you to attention, like a bucket of ice water flung in your face, letting you know unequivocally that you must walk away from a lifetime of self-abuse and inebriation or your life will be over? For Greg Myerson, the moment finally came during a weeklong stay with friends at a rental house on Block Island.

Although he had gone to rehab for a month after his fight with Brian Jackson several years earlier, his heart wasn't in it. He'd only agreed to it because his family told him if he didn't stop abusing alcohol and drugs, they wouldn't have anything more to do with him. But he loved to party, and he took it up again within weeks of finishing rehab. He could easily afford the drugs and alcohol with the money he earned as a union electrician.

During the Fourth of July week in 2001, Greg and six friends split the $10,000 rental fee for a magnificent place. Valued at more than $5 million and owned by a wealthy doctor, it had eight rooms, most with their own fireplaces and bathrooms. Greg got the master bedroom, with its own private balcony and hot tub. The rental period went from Saturday afternoon until the following Saturday morning, and they were planning for the final night there, on Friday, to be the party to end all parties. They had brought cases of liquor, wine, and beer, as well as plenty of pot and cocaine.

Greg and the others sharing the rental house were all journeyman union electricians and had been working for months at a power plant in Wallingford, Connecticut. They made excellent pay, but they were all being laid off as the project wound down.

Greg was thirty-three years old that summer and had been abusing drugs and alcohol since at least the age of fourteen. Many nights he'd put away a quart or more of Tanqueray gin or Jim Beam. In the months leading up to his stay at Block Island, while he was working at the power plant, Greg was partying harder than ever. On the days he wasn't fishing, he would often go straight from work to happy hour at a bar and still be drinking and dancing in his work clothes at 2:00 a.m. when the bar closed.

Maybe it was only a matter of time before this lifestyle took a toll on him. He had begun having bouts of deep anxiety—debilitating panic attacks unlike anything he'd ever experienced. One afternoon they were so bad, he just lay on his bed trembling and starting to hyperventilate. He finally jumped into his pickup truck and drove to the boat dock, seeking release from the stress he was feeling. In his agitation he didn't even check the fuel level or put any food or water on board.

It was midafternoon and the weather was still pleasant as he untied the ropes holding the boat to the cleats on the dock. He climbed aboard, fired up the motor, and began backing out. Five minutes later, he had cleared the jetty and was heading eastward with no destination in mind. It didn't matter. Nothing mattered. He didn't even look up later when he passed the Race or Block Island. Soon he felt the vast swells of the open ocean lifting his boat, pushing against it, but still he pushed on with the throttle forward, long after night fell, long after the last light visible on shore became a distant twinkle on the horizon and then blinked out. Sometime late in the night he ran out of fuel, then lay silently down in the bottom of the boat. The boat rocked quietly, occasionally slammed by a wave, but still he drifted seaward. Where would he end up? How long until his own light went out?

He drifted endlessly in the dark without the boat's green and red safety lights turned on. If any other vessel came blasting through in the steamer lanes they wouldn't even see him. But he was alone in the dark and the silence of the vast ocean. He thought back on his life, remembering everything—the people he'd known; the fish he'd caught; the women he'd loved; and the wild parties—all that wasted life. And then he fell into a fitful slumber.

Greg awoke the next day, sometime in the late morning, parched, sunburned, and hungry, the sun beating mercilessly down on him. Someone was shaking him, trying to rouse him. A commercial fisherman knelt over him, offering a drink of water as two of his shipmates tied a line from Greg's boat to the tuna boat they worked on. Greg never told them what he was up to, and they didn't ask. They towed him back to the closest port, in Rhode Island, then made their way back out to the open sea.

A short time later, Greg went to a doctor who prescribed the antianxiety medication Xanax. He started carrying it with him all the time in the hip pocket of his jeans, always ready to pop one in his mouth, crunching it up with his teeth so it would act more quickly. (He had previously always carried a dime bag of cocaine in his pocket, so it would be ready if he needed a boost.) The Xanax didn't solve his problem, but it eased it enough to let him go on with his routine.

So Greg was feeling good as he drove onto the Block Island ferry in his pickup truck, full of fishing gear, coolers of beer, and bottles of whiskey, vodka, gin, and wine. He started inviting people on the ferry to come to his big party the following Friday, hoping to get the word out to as many people as possible. His friend Jeff was already motoring to Block Island in his fishing boat, and the two met shortly after Greg came ashore. It was Friday, and too early to get into the rental house, so they ended up sleeping on the beach that first night. Greg was really looking forward to fishing. Early July was a good time to find striped bass in the far eastern stretch of Long Island Sound around Block Island, where the sound meets the open Atlantic, and he eagerly awaited the chance to get out in the boat the next morning. Although Greg was a dedicated partier when the sun went down, in the morning he was all business and wanted to catch fish.

"I was never someone who had to party all day," said Greg. "But I liked to have fun at night. My whole life was like that. Until I was in my late twenties, most people didn't even know that I partied."

Most of the week in Block Island was great. They went fishing every day and ate whatever they caught: fluke, striped bass, and more. Jeff, a diver, caught lobsters by the gunnysack-full every night, and they ate them for lunch, dinner—even breakfast, shredded into omelets. But the most spectacular catch of all was a magnificent striped bass Greg caught on a fly rod—almost by accident. He was standing on the jetty in front of the Spring House Hotel on the southeastern coast of Block Island, demonstrating to one of his friends the techniques of saltwater fly fishing. He was using a nine-weight saltwater fly rod, better for mid-sized fish, not huge stripers—and he had only a ten-pound tippet.

In fly fishing, the angler uses a thicker, heavier, plastic-coated woven line called a fly line. It's usually 70 to 100 feet long, and the weight of this line is what makes it possible to cast a virtually weightless fly long distances. We've all seen fly fisherman waving their rods back and forth like a magic wand, casting the fly line out behind them and forward again, finally dropping the fly gently down to the water. The way this works, the weight of the line as it's thrown behind you in the back cast bends the rod back so that on the forecast, all the energy released as the rod straightens out throws the line forward powerfully yet gently, so the fly drifts down to land softly on the water. At the front end of the fly line is several feet of monofilament leader—which is much thinner and less visible than the fly line—and at the end of the leader is a gossamer-thin length of monofilament called the tippet, which is virtually invisible to the fish. The back end of the fly line, where it goes into the reel, is usually attached to 100 yards of braided Dacron line, used as a backing in case a fish makes a powerful run and spools out all the fly line.

That morning, Greg was using an Epoxy Shiner fly, which floats on the surface and is designed to mimic a small, silvery baitfish. He cast it out into the surf and started stripping in line to impart a lifelike appearance to the fly. Then he paused and was pointing out some of the features of the fly reel to his friend, when suddenly *whomp!* —a massive explosion of water boiled up right where the fly had been, and the fight was on. The take was so fast and violent, the fish almost tore the fly rod out of Greg's hand, but he instantly calmed down, his instincts for the hunt switching on in his mind.

He knew it was a big fish, and he didn't want to lose it, but in seconds it had already peeled out all of the fly line and was deep into the backing. He jumped down from the jetty and began running full speed along the beach in the direction the fish was traveling, trying his best not to let it spool out all his line and break off. It was a great challenge. He knew the big striper was far too heavy for a ten-pound tippet, but that was what he had to work with, and he was determined to land this fish. His only hope was to slowly and carefully tire the fish out until he could pull it into the surf and get hold of it. In some ways, this was like the time he had chased the big buck up the mountain in Vermont in a snowstorm. There was no way he would quit. His entire being was in this fight. And it required all of his sensitivity as a fisherman: the feel for exactly how much tension to maintain on the line, when to let the fish run, and when to gently pull it toward him without ever using enough pressure to break the tippet.

He worked slowly and methodically, reeling in line every time the fish was moving in his direction, and letting out line again when it pulled frantically away. Three times he reeled in all of the backing and was working with the fly line again, and three times the fish peeled it out again—one time coming dangerously close to stripping all the line from the reel. And the fish kept changing directions. Greg had to keep running up and down the shoreline, tripping and falling a couple of times as he followed the fish in its struggle to escape. It was both exhilarating and exhausting, and more than an hour later, when he finally saw the fish come rolling into the surf, Greg was staggering from the unrelenting exertion—and he didn't have a net. With the last of his strength, he took a flying leap at the fish, like a football tackle, quickly getting hold of its lower jaw—but not before being poked by several of the spikes on the fish's back. He dragged the fish up onto the wet sand, panting from the exertion and bleeding from being spiked. His friend just shook his head in amazement.

"And that's how you catch a striped bass with a fly rod!" Greg told him.

The fish probably weighed well over forty pounds and might even have broken the world record for the largest striped bass ever caught with a fly rod. But back then, Greg had never even thought about trying to break records. He just loved to catch fish. They grilled the bass that evening, and it was plenty big enough to feed everyone and have leftovers.

The party on Friday night, their last night in the rental house, became a nightmare for Greg. Dozens of people showed up, and it was loud and raucous, with heavy drinking. But no one drank more than Greg. He'd been snorting cocaine, had finished off a quart of Tanqueray gin, and was starting in on a bottle of Jim Beam. Suddenly an intense pain gripped his chest, almost dropping him to his knees. He staggered a few feet, holding his hand against his chest and leaning hard against a wall to stay upright. He was gasping for air, incapable of drawing a deep breath—the pain was so deep and crushing and sharp. Greg has an incredible threshold for pain—all of his coaches, football teammates, and friends will tell you they've never known anyone who could tolerate as much pain as he can. But this was beyond anything he'd ever known, like a great dark pall was descending over him, and he felt he might not live until morning. Was it a heart attack? It could well have been. Although he was only thirty-three years old, he'd been abusing his body with drugs, alcohol, and cigarettes for more than half his life, and it was taking its toll.

Greg made his way painfully to the master bedroom and locked the door to keep the other partiers away. Throughout his life, he'd been drawn to water whenever he was having any kind of problems: he would go fishing, or sometimes just plunge into the ocean to swim. This time was no different, except that the only water available was the hot tub on his private porch. He climbed into the tub with his clothes still on. Sitting with steaming hot water right up to his chin, he prayed to God to help him. He swore that if he lived to see morning, he would change his ways—no drugs, no drinks, no cigarettes—cold turkey, just walking away from the life he'd known for almost twenty years.

He fell asleep right there in his sodden clothes, up to his neck in hot water. If he had slipped under or had any further heart complications, he probably would have drowned, and no one would have known about it until the next day. As it turned out, he awoke at midmorning to the shouts of an angry woman standing below the balcony where he still lay in the tub. The water had turned cold, and he was nearly hypothermic in the frigid tub. He no longer felt the excruciating pain in his chest, but he was nauseated and ached all over. Hauling himself out of the tub, he dragged himself to the railing, gallons of water pouring from his clothes. Convulsive surges gripped his body. Leaning far out over the rail, he spewed projectile vomit nearly ten feet out, barely missing the rental manager below, throwing up again and again until only bile came, followed by dry heaves.

The woman was furious. Greg and the others were supposed to have had the whole place cleaned out and ready to reoccupy by now. The next group of renters was due to arrive in a couple of hours, and the place was a shambles, with passed-out revelers sprawled everywhere amid empty bottles, cigarette butts, trash, and vomit. She called the police and had everyone thrown out. She threatened to take them to court and make them pay for all of the damage and cleanup as well as the next week's rental fee, because she was going to have to turn away the people who were arriving that day.

Greg was a wreck. He told his friend Jeff what had happened the night before and that there was no way he could drive back home for the next few days. His anxiety level was through the roof, and he was genuinely terrified. Jeff told him not to worry. He checked them into a cheap (for Block Island) motel, and the two stayed there another week before Greg felt comfortable enough to make the trip home.

When he got back to his apartment, Greg holed up there for weeks, barely even going outside into the yard. Finally, a couple he had met on Block Island telephoned and said they'd like to get together and take him out to dinner, but he told them he had bad anxiety and wasn't going out anymore. They dropped by his apartment later and saw what bad shape he was in. The woman said he should see a therapist as soon as possible, and she set up an appointment for him.

When he got to the therapist's office the following Tuesday morning, CNN was playing on the television in the waiting room, and it was all about something going on in Manhattan, a huge emergency of some kind, and one of the towers of the World Trade Center was on fire. As he watched aghast, a jetliner flew right into the second tower. It was September 11, 2001, and the terrorist attack unfolded on the screen before him.

By the time he was called in to see the therapist, Greg was in a major panic attack and having trouble catching his breath. She prescribed large doses of Xanax for anxiety and Paxil, a powerful antidepressant used to treat a host of problems such as depression, obsessive-compulsive disorder, social anxiety disorder, panic disorder, as well as post-traumatic stress disorder. It took a couple of weeks for the Paxil to have an effect, but when it did kick in fully, the difference was profound. He seemed to lose all of his desire to fight people or to hang out in bars and chase women. Instead, Greg dug deep into the essence of his life, returning to the things that had sustained him as a child—being close to nature; hunting and fishing. He was finally able to leave his apartment, after spending weeks alone there.

He had a good amount of money saved from all his work in the electrical union. Since he wasn't wasting it on partying and buying drugs and alcohol anymore, he began to turn his life around. He bought the house he'd been living in for several years and moved upstairs, renting out the basement where he had previously lived. He began to enjoy life in a way he'd forgotten was possible.

IT'S OVER

One morning Greg was sitting in a chair, watching the lobsters in his aquarium, when his mother dropped by. It was 2004, already three years since he'd turned away from abusing drugs and alcohol.

"I'll never forget that," he said. "I was sitting in my chair, staring at my fish tank, when she came up the stairs. She said, 'It's over,' and I knew instantly what she meant. My father was dead. And it was such a relief. The torture we'd all gone through, including my father—it didn't end right away, but it started fading. And I was on my way to becoming the person I always wanted to be."

Greg went to his parents' condo that same day and took all of his father's equipment for the disabled—his adjustable hospital bed, his special elevating chair, his wheelchair, and everything else he could find that reminded him of Herb's decades-long ordeal—and threw it out in the yard. Then he began smashing it with a sledgehammer, breaking it, bending it, crushing it until there was nothing left but a barely recognizable mass of bent and broken steel and plastic. His mother walked out as he was carrying the broken pieces to the dumpster and tossing them inside.

She frowned. "You know someone probably could have used those things." Greg stared straight ahead, expressionless. Then Diane's look softened. "But I can see how that might make you feel better."

Later, at Herb's funeral, Greg's brother was surprised to see how many people showed up. "I pulled in, and there were all these cars," said Dave. "I thought there must be two funerals going on, but no; it was all for my dad. There were all these mobster types who came to pay their respects. I'm standing there with my mother, and they're all going up to Greg. And my mother says, 'I feel like I'm in an episode of *The Sopranos*.' I said, 'I actually think we are.'"

"A lot of people came, all different kinds," said Greg. "They loved him and respected him."

Greg took his father's death well. Herb had been living such a tortured existence for so long—twenty years. Now his suffering was over. It had been a much different story a few years earlier when his maternal grandmother passed away, at the height of Greg's period of substance abuse. She had meant so much to him for his entire life. He'd gone to see her whenever he couldn't get along with his mother and stayed with her for months at a time.

"We were always really close," said Greg. "She taught me how to pray. Every morning when I woke up, she'd have toast with butter and jelly and tea for me. She'd be praying in the living room, and I'd sit there and pray with her. That's what we did every morning. When she died, it was one of the worst things in my life."

Greg was to be one of her pallbearers. The night before the funeral, he had pulled an all-nighter with some friends, drinking and snorting coke until the early hours of morning. It was a cold, gray, miserable winter day, with a mix of sleet, snow, and rain falling steadily. His friend Brad drove Greg to his house to get ready. He put on his dress clothes but no jacket, and Brad dropped him off at the funeral home.

"I stumbled inside and broke down," said Greg. He was an absolute mess, crying uncontrollably for hours. His mother, his brother, and other people kept trying to console him so the funeral could proceed, but he sat in a chair along the side, his head buried in his hands, and wouldn't look up. When it was all over, he and the other pallbearers picked up her casket and carried it outside. Everyone else had dressed appropriately for the weather, wearing raincoats or overcoats. Greg wore only a thin dress shirt with no T-shirt underneath, and leather dress shoes, as he stood in the slushy snow, wet from head to foot.

"No one else was as affected as I was at that funeral—not my mother, not anyone," said Greg. "My grandmother and I had such a close relationship. I was always with her."

But Herb's death was not a sorrowful event for Greg, or for anyone who had witnessed his suffering in the final years of his life. Now he would never have to hear his father pleading with him, begging him to take that pillow and hold it down on his face until he was dead. Greg shuddered to remember it, and he felt an immense sense of relief, like a great weight had been lifted from him.

ARROWHEAD

Life was good now. Greg owned his own home, he had some money in the bank—and he had met a woman named Jackie. She lived next door with her two young sons from a previous marriage, and Greg loved to hang out with all of them. Eventually he and Jackie got married, had a daughter together, and bought a beautiful, spacious home in Wallingford.

It was a dream house for both of them, with wooded hills full of deer behind and a stream in front. When they first moved in, Greg rented a backhoe to enlarge and deepen the stretch of stream flowing past the front of the house, and moved boulders around to improve the fish habitat. Several decent-sized trout soon took up residence there. He didn't fish there though. The trout in his stream were almost like pets to him: something to watch and enjoy. Occasionally he'd flip a grasshopper into the water and watch with delight as it got hammered by a big trout.

Yet something was missing. Greg couldn't quite put his finger on it. He had fully embraced the nine-to-five life, working hard to support

his family and maintain their home. But still, he felt a sense of empti-
ness and anxiety.

As he had done many times before throughout his life, he turned
to nature for solace and went hiking in the woods behind his house. It
was early fall, and he felt the change in seasons keenly—the chill air;
the brilliant blaze of autumn colors spreading orange, red, and yellow
through the woods; and, above all, the urge to hunt. It was rutting time
and signs of deer abounded in the woods he hiked through: scrapes in
the ground where bucks had urinated to announce their presence, like
a gauntlet thrown down in challenge, and gouges in the bark of trees
where they had been rubbing the velvet off their antlers, in prepara-
tion for their fights with other bucks competing to mate with does. He
paused by one tree and put his hand on the remarkably large gouges in
its bark. *This buck is huge*, he thought. He imagined it: an eight-pointer,
perhaps weighing close to 300 pounds.

Greg went home and fetched a deer stand. He climbed a tree ad-
jacent to one the big buck had been rubbing against and attached the
stand securely to its trunk, about twenty feet up. Greg would climb up
to it dressed head-to-foot in camouflage before dawn on opening day of
deer season and wait . . . and wait, hoping the buck would return.

He continued his hike through the woods. He hadn't gone far when
he spotted a small, shiny object glistening in the early morning light,
half buried. He reached down and plucked it from the hard ground. It
was a stone arrowhead, and he turned it over a couple of times in his
hand, examining the perfection of its form, still razor-sharp after lying
there perhaps for centuries. He imagined the hunter who had crafted it
so long ago and wondered what his life had been like.

Greg had been fascinated since childhood by stories of the Native
Americans who had lived in this area when the Europeans first arrived
in the early 1600s. The coastal Algonquian, called Quinnipiac, inhab-
ited all of what is now New Haven, North Haven, Hamden, Branford,
Guilford, and the surrounding area, and had taught the English settlers

how to hunt and fish to survive the harsh winters. The forebears of the Quinnipiac had lived there for some 8,000 years. Sadly, they fell victim to smallpox and other imported diseases, which quickly reduced their populations by more than 75 percent. Only a handful of Quinnipiac remained by the time of the founding of the United States, and by 1850 —according to John William De Forest, who wrote *The History of the Indians of Connecticut* that year—the Quinnipiac no longer existed as a tribe.

If you trace the boundaries of Greg's life—where he grew up, where he developed as an outdoorsman, and where he lives and hunts and fishes to this day—they match the tribal lands of the Quinnipiac almost exactly. And he always felt their presence. As a child, he would find their arrowheads and stone implements for grinding acorn meal, and be in awe. He longed to be like them—to fish, trap, and hunt deer. He imagined what it must have been like for them, living in this paradise for millennia before European civilization came to these shores and changed everything forever.

Another person might have kept the arrowhead as a talisman, perhaps something to be worn around the neck in a pouch. Not Greg. His mind went immediately to hunting: to building an arrow around it; to hunting with that single arrow and killing the giant buck with it. He'd already been a bow-hunter since his early twenties and had killed many deer with arrows, but they were always modern, aluminum-shafted arrows tipped with razor-sharp metal broadheads. He'd never done it like a Native American.

Greg searched for straight willow branches, just like the ones the Quinnipiac had used, because of their strength and flexibility. He cut them from trees growing along the stream in front of his house, whittled them down to the right size, and tested their straightness by rolling them along a flat surface. Some of them wobbled, indicating they were slightly bent. But one of them was perfectly straight, and he chose it for his arrow, notching its tip and lashing the arrowhead securely in place with a thin strip of buckskin. He put feathers on the shaft to steady its flight and drew a design on it using natural colors. By the time it was finished, the arrow looked like a museum piece crafted by a Native American a couple of centuries or more ago.

As he was about to leave his house in the early morning darkness of opening day, Greg put the arrow he'd made into his quiver, along with several aluminum-shafted arrows. But then he paused. He knew if he took the other arrows with him, he'd end up using one of them instead when he saw the deer, and it would ruin the experience. The arrow he'd made with the ancient arrowhead was the thing that would make this hunt special, and he was determined to kill the buck with it. He removed all the other arrows from his quiver, then picked up his bow, went outside, and hiked through the woods to his tree stand.

"I got up in the tree and started rattling a couple of antlers together," said Greg. The buck showed up instantly, snorting and stomping, enraged by this perceived challenger in his territory. Greg was taken aback by the size of the buck. "He was a monster, almost 300 pounds, pissed off and ready to fight," he said.

Would he really be able to kill it with the wooden arrow he'd carved? He began doubting himself. Above all, he didn't want the buck to escape wounded and endure a long, lingering death. So he waited . . . and waited as it slowly came closer. When it was just ten feet away, he drew back on the bow, inhaling deeply and holding his breath as he carefully aimed. His mind was absolutely locked in the moment, everything in his being focused on the bow, the arrow, and the deer—and then with a *whoosh* the arrow flew to its target. The buck lifted his head at the sound and bolted as it struck.

"I shot him right in the heart with the arrow," said Greg. "It didn't pass through, but went right in and killed him almost instantly. He only ran maybe thirty or forty yards, and then fell dead to the ground."

When Greg gutted the deer a short time later, he found that the arrow had pierced the buck's heart, so it bled to death nearly instantly. Greg kept the arrow—this was the only time he ever used it—and it still has the blood of the great buck on it. He dressed out the buck and ate all of its meat and mounted its head himself. It now hangs on the wall of his house, and it is magnificent.

TOURNAMENT ANGLER

Something changed for Greg after he killed the buck with the ancient arrowhead. He felt a deep sense of inspiration. All the things that had moved him as a child—the deep need to be close to nature: the hunting, fishing, and trapping—came flooding back, and he began spending every free moment engaged in these pursuits. He was as much or more obsessed with them as he had ever been in his life.

The following summer, in 2010, was a life-changer for Greg. He was fishing most nights, catching some of the largest striped bass he'd ever hooked. And he was releasing most of them. In a lifetime of fishing for stripers, he had come to greatly admire them. He loved the challenge of outsmarting them, drawing them in with the rattle sinker he'd designed and catching them using the techniques he had perfected. But he felt no desire to kill them—he simply enjoyed the hunt, and preferred to set them free once he'd caught them.

He usually bought eels and other bait at Jack's Shoreline Bait and Tackle in Westbrook, Connecticut, which attracted a broad cross-section of striped bass fishermen, ranging from the ultrawealthy to those who might not have two nickels to rub together. Here they met as equals to hang out and talk about the fish all of them pursued so avidly. The place felt like a relic from the early 1900s. Some of the top striped bass fishermen on the Eastern Seaboard frequented the shop. Greg found himself spending more and more of his free time at Jack's —at least the time when he wasn't out fishing. He enjoyed hanging around with others who shared his keen love of striped bass fishing.

The shop happened to be an official weighing station for the Striper Cup, the largest tournament of its kind in the Northeast, sponsored each year by *On the Water* magazine and attracting thousands of competitors. Jack Katzenbach, the owner of the shop, knew what a great striped bass fisherman Greg was and one day told him: "You catch bigger fish day in and day out than any of these guys. You should enter the Striper Cup."

The tournament lasts nearly five months each year, from May 1 to September 15, and it had already been going on for more than a month, so everyone had a huge head start on Greg. He had never before even thought about entering a tournament, but: *What the hell*, he thought. *Why not?* And as with everything he does, Greg was all in. He started going out every night, in all kinds of weather—and Long Island Sound can have remarkably brutal conditions, with deadly storms sweeping into the area in a matter of minutes. It didn't matter to Greg; he was out there braving the roughest seas when everyone else stayed home.

Greg usually fished either alone or with Brian Beauchamp, a fellow electrician who had gone through the union apprenticeship with him. The two later worked together at the Connecticut Department of Transportation, doing electrical work and also driving snowplows in winter. It was Brian who got Greg his job at the DOT. When they fished together, they would net each other's fish or steer the boat when one of them had a fish on.

Late one night that June they were fishing in Long Island Sound, repeatedly drifting over Southwest Reef (where he later caught his world-record striped bass). It was a rough night, with gale-force winds blowing in from the north, throwing up vast sheets of water, turning Long Island Sound into a seething cauldron of churning sea. Suddenly Greg felt a fish take the bait, and he set the hook hard. The high-pitched scream of the reel pierced the night as the fish stripped out yard after yard of line. He knew it would soon clean out his reel and break off. His only chance was to move the boat in the direction the fish was swimming and try to reel in as much of the line as he could before it was all gone. This sometimes happens to shore fishermen when they hook a huge fish, and it starts peeling away all of their line. About all they can do is increase the tension on the line and hope for the best. But in a boat you can follow the fish's escape path and try to keep up with it, reeling in the line as you make your way closer. The problem on this night, though, was that he couldn't see which direction the fish was moving. The night was pitch black, with the wind howling across the sea, blowing saltwater spray into his face, stinging his eyes. And the fish had taken off like a rocket.

Brian held a spotlight on the fishing line so Greg could drive toward it, but it was hard—Greg was driving and reeling at the same time, trying his best to gain back the line the fish had peeled out. He didn't want to blow it. He knew the fish was huge, maybe the biggest one he'd ever hooked, and he was determined to land it.

After nearly an hour of fighting, Greg sensed the fish was coming near. He nodded to Brian, who picked up the landing net and stood ready while the boat rose up and down in the storm-tossed sea and they both struggled to stay on their feet. As the striper came into view, Brian deftly slipped the net underneath it and hoisted it up into the boat.

The fish tipped the scales at sixty-nine pounds—at that point, the largest striped bass ever caught in the history of the Striper Cup. No one had even caught a sixty-pounder in the tournament before. Amazingly, Greg caught two more fish that topped sixty pounds before the Striper Cup was over. For this, he won Angler of the Year and Striped Bass of the Year.

To put Greg's accomplishment in perspective: in the more than a century sport fishermen have been recording the size of the large game fish they catch, fewer than 100 striped bass have been caught that weighed sixty pounds or more. Tony Checko, author of *The Striped Bass 60+ Pound Club*, interviewed Greg shortly after his tournament win and told him he didn't need to catch a world-record striped bass to be a famous fisherman; catching three sixty-plus pounders in a year was far more impressive than the world record set by Albert McReynolds. At that time, Greg had never even heard of McReynolds or the world-record striped bass he had caught one stormy night in 1982 from a stone jetty on the New Jersey coast—a record that had stood for nearly three decades.

Greg was a huge sensation at that year's StriperFest—the East Coast's biggest fishing party, held each year at the conclusion of the Striper Cup. He had never attended the event before and was amazed how many people showed up and the adulation they showered on him.

"There's ten thousand people, and you're the guy," he said. The tournament officials presented him with a mount of the biggest fish he'd caught, and he held it high above his head, doing a "fish pump." He was the first person to do that, and the crowd loved it. Greg enjoyed the attention of the people at StriperFest and loved talking to them and telling them stories. He knew he'd be back again. His life as a tournament angler had begun.

For his family life, though, it was a different story.

ONE MORE DRIFT

Fishing has ended a lot of relationships for Greg. No one could put up with his obsession for the long haul. His wife, Jackie, lasted the longest, three years, and they had a daughter together. It had started off so great. Jackie even liked to fish — but that was true of a number of women he'd been involved with over the years.

"Some of them said they enjoyed fishing, or even loved it," said Greg. "But not my kind of fishing. Their attitude would change when things got rough. I fish through anything. As soon as they got a taste of that they'd realize, 'I'm on the verge of dying out here.' And they were like, 'You're sick!'"

Greg took Jackie fishing with him a lot when they first got together. But she was a nurse and had to work nights, so after a couple of hours she'd say, "We need to leave now. I have to get to work." And Greg would invariably reply, "All right, just one more drift," and he'd drive the boat all the way back around and let the current slowly carry them over the reef again . . . and again . . . and again, saying, "One more drift. One more drift."

"I would make her late for work, and she'd freak out, calling me a motherfucker all the way home. 'Well don't come with me then,' I'd say. 'You don't want to fish anyway, what the fuck.' No one wants to do it the way I do it. No one *can* do it the way I do it. It got to where my closest friends wouldn't fish with me anymore. When they wanted to leave, they couldn't. I only left when I was ready to leave, which was hardly ever."

And Greg never thought to bring food or something to drink on his fishing excursions. One time, when the stripers were moving through, he went out with only one small Gatorade on board and fished three entire tides—that's eighteen hours. Going out for some quick fishing, a couple of casts, just doesn't happen with Greg. If the fish are biting, he doesn't stop unless he's out of bait or gas or the boat is sinking.

"So much shit has happened to me out there," said Greg. "I'm out there at night, all by myself, running on empty, and the fish are biting, so I fish until I run out of gas. I know that's not normal, but that's the way I am."

Jackie was on the boat with Greg one stormy night in Long Island Sound, tossed by wind and waves and torrential rain, when the motor sputtered and died. And they sat there as the rain poured down on them endlessly—sheets of it, buckets of it, drenching them until they were sodden from head to foot. Jackie was furious. Greg's old friend Verne Carlson and a couple of other people finally came out to rescue them, and as they pulled up, Greg had just hooked a striper. "Look at him, he's fucking crazy," said Verne, laughing. "He's got a fish on."

Things only went downhill from there. "You're not going fishing tonight," Jackie would scream as he was putting his fishing rods in the truck. "Shut up!" he'd say. And it would go back and forth: "I hate you! Don't come back!" "Good, I won't!" And he would be off, braving the foulest weather alone in the roughest seas: one more drift . . . one more drift.

One day in the late afternoon, he saw a horrendous storm speeding toward him, with black skies, high winds, and crashing claps of thunder and lightning. But the fish were biting, so he stayed, pushing himself to endure beyond all bounds of common sense and reason, finally having to flee for his life at full throttle as the storm came sweeping like a tempest across the sound. He was in a small open boat and had to find shelter immediately.

"I could barely make it into the first marina," said Greg. "There was an abandoned boat, a forty-footer, in dry storage there. I lifted up the hatchway, barely big enough to fit through, and climbed inside. The storm blasted through, dropping golf-ball-sized hail. I would've been dead if I didn't make it to shelter in time."

The funny part is, Greg had been watching the storm moving in from the distance for an hour. He could have made it all the way back to his own marina and been driving home by the time it hit. But the fishing was too good for him to stop.

Jackie called him on his cell phone as he lay huddled in the derelict boat, waiting for the storm to pass. "There's no way you're fishing in this," she said, suspiciously. "What are you really doing?" Greg just hung up on her. As soon as the weather cleared, he motored back out into Long Island Sound—the deck of his boat still covered with icy slush from sleet and hailstones—and started fishing again.

Greg and Jackie's marriage didn't end overnight. It wasn't like there was one last straw. "There was a lot of straw," said Greg. If you look at the arc of Greg's life from a relationship standpoint, this was as good as it gets. This was the time when he almost made it work—but then it didn't.

He'd pushed relationships far beyond the breaking point many times before. There was Rebecca, a woman he met and fell in love with one winter. They soon moved in together. Greg spent the cold winter months tying trout flies, which Rebecca found quaint. She had no idea of the extent of his interest in fishing and that what he was doing was building an arsenal of flies for the upcoming trout season. As soon as spring arrived, he pretty much disappeared, going fly fishing every night after work on the Salmon River, an hour's drive away.

"After work I would just shoot up there and fish till nine o'clock, when it got dark, and be home at midnight," said Greg. "Then I worked all day. So a month went by, and all I heard was shit. I kept buying all kinds of fishing gear. I had so many rods."

Then one Saturday morning Rebecca asked, "Where you going?"

"I'm going fishing."

She left the bedroom, and Greg thought she was in the bathroom. Then he heard loud crashing and crunching sounds coming from the driveway.

"I looked out the window, and all my stuff was piled up: my fishing vest, my boots, my rods—all kinds of rods, not just fly rods, *all* of my rods," said Greg. "And she was running over them, going back and forth with her car."

She finally came inside and said, "Well, it looks like you can't go fishing. So now what are we going to do?"

"You forgot the rod I always keep on the dashboard of my truck," he said. He walked outside and climbed into his pickup.

"If you go fishing, don't ever come back!" she said.

"And that was the end of it," said Greg. "I just cleaned out my stuff and left. I never saw her again."

Greg is not without self-awareness: far from it. He's a very sensitive person. His brother Dave, Aunt Cookie, Bear, and virtually everyone else I interviewed told me that. It's just that he is so dedicated to his passions, it's hard for him to give enough time to someone else to sustain a relationship. Even the women in Greg's life who've had an interest in hunting and fishing could never comprehend how far he was willing to go to catch that fish or shoot that big buck, facing frigid temperatures, treacherous seas, and endless untold dangers on drift after drift, night after night, trip after trip . . . never resting, never stopping, not even to take a drink of water. It makes a person hard. Greg knows that.

"The last thing I ever want to hear is that you want to go home, you've had enough, you're scared or cold, or you have to go to work in the morning!" said Greg, then paused wistfully. "It seems like everyone who ever mattered in my life has just been broken down by me to the point of no return. I've ruined many relationships because of my self-ishness. I've hurt so many people who just wanted to be with me . . . people who actually loved me. And I always used to think *they* were the ones being selfish. Who were *they* to stop me from doing what I loved so much? Why should I conform to what *they* want? And I *have* tried. I've sat through their events and pretended to like their friends, when I was actually sizing their friends up and not being able to comprehend how soft some of them were. And comparing these people to what I can endure or enjoy is not good for a healthy relationship. And they all fail. But the great loves of my life never leave my mind, even though they're gone forever. I have not stopped loving any of them."

Greg and Jackie are still officially married, but they haven't lived together since the spring of 2011. They see each other briefly every weekend when he comes to pick up his daughter Jenny on Friday night and returns her home on Sunday night. His relationship with Jenny is the most important thing in his life.

"My daughter Jenny just turned ten years old, and my views on life, especially my life, have started to change," said Greg. "She stays with me on the weekends, and I look forward to seeing and spending time with her. I pray to God every day for her safety, sometimes two or three times a day. I live my life now thinking twice about some of the situations I don't have to put myself in. I have never loved anyone or anything more than her. She has changed everything about me and the way I see the world."

Jenny has had a huge impact in Greg's life. He's no longer as quick to make rash decisions that might put his life at risk, and he's less likely to get into a fight if he's provoked. He often takes her fishing with him, though never in dangerous conditions. In 2012, when Jenny was five years old, she won top honors in the annual North Haven Trout Derby, catching a whopping twenty-inch trout. Greg had won the same event in 1975 at age seven.

"I'm not so hungry to kill myself to catch a fish anymore," said Greg. "Everything I do now is because of her. If she wasn't around, I probably wouldn't be alive today. My luck was bound to run out sometime."

ANATOMY OF A
WORLD-RECORD CATCH

Greg hadn't even planned to go fishing on that Thursday night, August 4, 2011. He'd been fishing hard for more than a week, going out right after work and not getting home till the early hours of morning. And his friend Brian Beauchamp, who fished with Greg almost every night, couldn't go that day. It was his birthday, and he planned to spend it with his wife, whom he had only recently married. Instead, it was Matt Farina who talked him into going fishing. He's an old friend who grew up in North Haven but went to another high school. Now a professional painter, he had been painting Greg's house and had gone fishing with Greg only a couple of times, most recently earlier that week. But he had become completely hooked since Greg taught him some techniques that boosted his fishing skills.

"I took him out and showed him the way I do it, and he was catching some really nice fish," said Greg. "He really wanted to go out fishing again." And of course it never takes much encouragement to get Greg to go. At the end of the day, they were on their way, driving to Greg's boat, with Matt still in his paint clothes.

It was a beautiful evening, with a first-quarter moon visible over-head and flat-calm seas, at dead high tide, slacking out—a perfect time to fish. Although it was nearly 8:00 p.m., the sun was still out, hover-ing just above the horizon, flooding the evening with rich golden light, dazzling like a thousand diamonds as it touched the water.

"That first-quarter moon is when I always like to fish," said Greg. "I'd been crushing it all week long, catching some big fish."

Greg headed out to Southwest Reef, his favorite reef in Long Is-land Sound, and got all of his equipment ready. He whacked an eel against the boat's gunwale to stun it, then pushed the hook through it just below its head. The rattle sinker was already attached about a foot and a half from the eel. When they were ready, Greg began mo-toring toward the reef, then cut the motor and let the boat's momen-tum drift them slowly onward. He and Matt lowered their eels over the side, running their lines out until they touched bottom, then reel-ing back so the bait would hang a foot or so above the rocks as they passed over the reef. As they drifted above the huge boulder where big fish often hang out, Greg felt a hard strike and jerked up on the rod to set the hook.

"When I yanked it, I'm sure I pulled it right out of her mouth," said Greg. "I could tell she never even touched the hook. I just know the feeling when they grab the back of the eel. They clamp onto it hard, and when you pull it, it feels like you have them for a second, then it pulls out of their mouth."

Greg could tell it was a very good fish, so he was careful how he set up for the next drift, taking the boat wide, in a huge circle, completely avoiding the spot where the big bass was feeding as he moved the boat into place for his next drift. Then they slowly drifted back over the exact spot again. Greg felt two big taps and set the hook hard. It felt like it was stuck in the rocks, but Greg knew better. Matt was doubtful.

"That's not a fish," he said. "You're hooked on the bottom."

"You're wrong, man. That is definitely a fish . . . a monster."

Greg had been having a lot of trouble lately getting snagged in lobster pots that commercial fishermen had put in this reef, right in the best places to drift for striped bass. But he'd recently straightened out the situation. He started pulling up the lobster pots from these prime areas and moving them to deeper water right before he went fishing each day, to the deep chagrin of the lobsterman who owned them. Then one day, a week before this trip, the lobsterman was waiting for him at the parking lot in front of Jack's Shoreline Bait and Tackle when he came in from fishing. They had a brief fistfight, after which they came to an understanding: the man would no longer put lobster pots in Greg's prime fishing areas.

Sunset was fast approaching when Greg hooked the fish. The bass stayed down for maybe ten minutes, then came shooting up, making a huge splash as it breached the surface, scattering water twenty feet in all directions. Its spiked dorsal fin looked almost like a cape, glistening spectacularly in the last rays of golden light as the sun touched the horizon.

"I thought, *that is a huge fish*," said Greg. "It was just massive, and it was pulling the boat. The tide was coming in really slowly, and the fish was running with the tide toward Madison, a town over. It pulled the boat about a mile."

At the end of the fight, more than thirty minutes later, Greg brought the fish alongside and Matt attempted to net it, but it saw the boat and shot right back down to the bottom, pulling the line under the boat. Afraid the line might break against the gunwale, Greg rushed over to the side to try to hold the rod out away from the boat, but he slipped on some eel slime and fell hard, smashing his ribs against the gunwale. (This was the exact spot where he always hit the eels to stun them, so it was very slimy there.)

When Greg finally brought the fish alongside again, Matt netted it against the swim platform and tried to haul it up, but the net snagged on the platform. The huge striper thrashed frantically as Matt struggled to untangle the net. When it finally came loose, he tried to raise it from the water, but the net handle wasn't up to the task.

"Matt tried to lift the net horizontally, and the handle started to bend," said Greg. "With a big fish like that, you need to pull it straight up and lift it in. I grabbed the side of the net with one hand and helped him haul it into the boat." But Greg had no complaints about Matt. "He did a really great job netting that fish. It wasn't easy."

Greg knew right away that it was the biggest striped bass he'd ever caught, but he had no idea it might be a world record. He'd never really thought about such things, but he did know this would completely shake up the standings in the Striper Cup. Less than a month and a half earlier, on June 19, Peter Vican had caught a striped bass weighing a staggering seventy-seven pounds, four ounces, off Block Island and looked like a shoo-in to win top honors in the tournament. Vican's fish was then the second-largest striper ever caught by a sport fisherman. But Greg's fish would definitely take over the top spot now and almost certainly be the winner.

Greg had a fish hold in the front of his boat that would usually easily accommodate any fish he kept. But he had to bend this fish to get it inside. And then he did something no other tournament angler would even think about doing if they'd caught a monster fish: he kept fishing—for hours. He and Matt had basically just gotten out there when Greg caught the fish, and there was no way they were going back to shore. So they spent all evening out there and caught and released several more nice fish, including the largest striper Matt had ever landed. From time to time throughout the evening, Greg would start wondering if the fish was as large as it seemed, and he'd go open the fish hold and look at it again. *Yep, it really is that big,* he'd think, then go back to fishing.

Unfortunately, their handling of this enormous bass was a near-textbook case of what not to do if you catch a potential world-record fish. The main concern is getting it to a weigh station as soon as possible, because it will start dehydrating and losing weight almost immediately. But then, even after hours of fishing, instead of trying to have the fish weighed, they went out to celebrate. After tying up the boat in front of Bill's Seafood in Westbrook, Greg laid the fish on the dock so everyone in the restaurant and bar could see it and take pictures. He and Matt stayed there till the bar closed. The fish easily could have lost three or four pounds or more in that time.

"It didn't fit in my cooler, so it hung around outside all night," said Greg. "I weighed it on a cheap digital scale at home, and it was eighty-three pounds, but it was probably more like eighty-five."

When he saw how much it weighed, Greg called and left a message on the answering machine at Jack's Shoreline Bait and Tackle saying that he had caught an eighty-three-pound striped bass and would be coming there in the morning to have it officially weighed. Then he dropped, exhausted, across his bed and fell into a deep sleep, leaving the fish in the back of his pickup truck until midmorning—and it was a warm morning. Most tournament anglers would have covered it with wet towels, doing everything possible to reduce the fish's dehydration.

By the time Greg woke up, news about the giant striper was already blazing up and down the East Coast. Between Jack calling a few people and some of the patrons at Bill's Seafood putting up pictures of Greg's fish, the word was out. Even though there had not yet been an official weighing, fishermen, newspaper reporters, magazine writers, and even someone from the popular *Good Morning America* television show flooded Jack's shop first thing in the morning. But Greg was a no-show, still sound asleep at home. Jack phoned him again and again to no avail.

Greg had the Weather Station on in the background as he was getting dressed and brushing his teeth, and he heard the TV reporter mention that a world-record striped bass had been caught the night before off Connecticut. He had no idea she was talking about him.

"I was thinking, *Wow, there must be some really big fish around*, as I was gargling and spitting out my mouthwash," said Greg.

By the time Greg got to Jack's shop, most of the media had given up and left. About a dozen fishermen had lingered on, hoping to see the fish. Greg still felt exhausted. He dropped the fish off with Jack, saying,

"Here, do what you gotta do," and went outside to get some fresh air. He hadn't gone far when he was hit by a wave of nausea and vomited in the parking lot of a Jet Ski dealership. A woman inside saw him and brought him a wet towel to clean himself off.

"You're Greg Myerson, aren't you?" she asked.

"Yes."

"You just caught the world-record striped bass."

Greg was dumbfounded. "I just looked at her and said, 'What are you talking about?'" After that, he went back to get his fish. A lot of people had returned to the shop by then to see it, but Greg just picked it up and started to leave.

"Hey, Greg. That fish weighed 81.88 pounds," said Jack. "You should wait. A photographer from On the Water magazine is on his way here."

Greg shrugged and said he was taking it to Rick Newberg's house just down the street. Jack called Rick a few minutes later and said, "Don't let Greg leave." He explained that the photographer was there and wanted to take pictures of Greg and the fish for a big feature article in the magazine. Rick tried to get Greg to stay, but he refused.

"Fuck them. I feel like shit. I'm out of here," said Greg as he climbed into his pickup truck.

But Rick was adamant. "This is important," he said. "You can't go anywhere." He got in front of Greg's truck and wouldn't budge.

"Get the fuck out of my way!"

At that instant, the photographer pulled into his driveway. Greg finally agreed to let him take a few pictures of him holding up his potential world-record striped bass. It was still only *potential* because catching a fish like that is only the first step on the road to having it recognized as a world record.

AFTERMATH

Walter Anderson barely knew Greg when he caught the world-record striped bass. He'd seen him a couple of times at Jack's Shoreline Bait and Tackle and once been regaled there by one of his great fishing stories. The first time they met, he and Greg and several other anglers were sitting around the shop, talking about past fishing adventures.

"I remember he was telling a story about the San Juan River of New Mexico," said Walter. The river is an incredibly beautiful, breathtaking place and has a special significance for Walter: it was where he caught the three largest trout of his life.

"Greg told a great story about how he and his football buddy were fishing in a drift boat with a local guide," said Walter. "His friend kept hooking him in the ear with a fly on his back casts, so Greg ended up punching him and getting into a big brawl. So this poor guide in the boat, he's got these two enormous guys, two football players, fighting in his drift boat. I got the biggest kick out of that story."

He told Greg they should go fishing together in Walter's boat, which he often takes to Block Island and other striped bass hotspots, and they agreed they'd do it sometime. But the next time Walter heard about

Greg was when Jack Katzenbach, who owned the bait shop, called on the morning of August 5, 2011, and told him Greg Myerson had caught a striped bass the night before that weighed eighty-two pounds. Walter almost dropped the phone.

"That's a world record," he said.

"Yeah, I know," said Jack. "I've got a bunch of people coming here. The phone's been ringing off the hook, and some of it is real nasty." He asked Walter if he'd mind coming down to the shop to give him advice on how to handle all the phone calls and media attention Greg's record-breaking bass was attracting. Walter is a renowned expert in the communications field. He had a lengthy career as a journalist and author and for many years was editor (and later CEO and chairman) of *Parade*, a popular weekly magazine appearing each Sunday in some 700 newspapers across the United States.

Jack also hoped Walter could give some advice to Greg, who had quickly gone from the early euphoria of catching such a huge fish into a deep funk. This was no doubt partly from exhaustion—but he'd also started having deep regrets about killing such a magnificent fish just to win a tournament.

"When I thought of everything that fish went through in her life— all those years facing the dangers of migrations, nor'easters, red tides, and pollution—and here I am, I wiped it out," he said. "It's bittersweet. People think it's just a fish, but it's a lot more than that to me." And worse, from Greg's standpoint, he killed the fish because he was competing in the Striper Cup and needed to catch a huge fish to overtake Peter Vican and win. Any other time, he would have released it in an instant.

"I've always had a lot of respect for the great fish I've caught, and I usually let them go. My friends would look at me like, 'What the hell are you doing?' But I'd put a huge striper over the side because it was awesome, and I'd think, *Why kill it?* I feel strongly about that."

He didn't care that the striper he caught that evening might be a world-record fish. It was a beautiful, pristine, spectacular striped bass

—just the kind of fish whose genes should be passed along to the next generation.

"A twenty-pound bass lays about 400,000 eggs a year," Greg told me, "but this one would lay six, seven, eight *million* eggs." Viewed in that way, her death was an immense loss to the native East Coast striped bass population, which is currently in serious decline.

On top of his personal regrets about killing the fish, Greg also had to face an onslaught of vicious rumors about his world-record catch— that somehow it had all been faked. Walter invited Greg to his home, and they had a long talk about the situation.

"I would say he was pretty close to depression within twenty-four hours of catching that fish," said Walter. "He went from an extraordinary high to a depression."

Greg could never have anticipated all the phone calls that would come flooding in from people trying to get in touch with him about the fish. Sadly, many of the calls were from people who were disputing the validity of his catch or just trying to insult him.

"Look, I don't need this," he told Walter. "I've got a job. I've got things to do. I'll go back and fish tonight." And Greg actually did go fishing the next night. When he got to the reef where he'd caught the enormous striper, boats were lined up virtually wall-to-wall there, with dozens of anglers eager to beat his accomplishment. No one was catching much. Greg casually drifted across the reef, caught a sixty-pounder, and released it in front of everyone.

There was always a significant chance that Greg would just say to hell with it and give up his claim to the world record. He didn't care about such things. He just wanted to go fishing.

The conspiracy theorists had had an instant field day with Greg's world-record claim—the fix was in; the scale it was weighed on was rigged; the fish had been stuffed with lead sinkers to raise its weight; or, most outrageous of all, a trawler had scooped the fish up in its net and sold it to Greg.

"Can you imagine?" said Walter. "It was all so preposterous. That fish was absolutely legitimate. So I talked to Greg about it and tried to settle him down. He was so upset. He just wanted it to go away. He told me, 'To hell with the fish, I'm going fishing.' But I wasn't going to let that happen. There was no doubt that this was the world record, and I wanted him to get credit for it. I told him, 'No, no, no, no! You spent a lifetime learning how to fish. You're one of the best fishermen in the country. Do not walk away from this.'"

Walter told me it was hard for him to contain his own temper, and he may well have given up if it had been his own record he was defending. But he had come to like and admire Greg, and he was determined he would get the recognition he deserved.

"In some ways, he was almost like a little brother or a son to me," he said. "I felt he was a really good guy, and he needed help."

Walter took Greg step-by-step through the application process for filing a fishing world record with the International Game Fish Association. With a record as important as the All-Tackle World Record for the largest striped bass, it was important to get it right.

"Just tell me the story chronologically from the beginning to the end, exactly what happened," Walter told him. "There's no detail that's too insignificant." He jotted it all down, helped Greg fill out the world-record application, and sent it to the IGFA.

Walter told him never to embellish the story of how he caught the fish. "Never forget the attorney's dictum, 'Truth is the unassailable defense,'" he said. "Just tell the truth. Here's what you want to beware of: when we start to tell a story, the first time we tell the truth, the second time we add a little point, the third time we begin to exaggerate. Don't do that. Always tell the story exactly as it occurred." He also warned him that reporters and writers might add their own embellishments when they tell his story, and if their accounts are too outrageous he should write to them and say, "I did not say that, I said this," and keep a record of it.

Walter encouraged him to ignore what other people might be saying about him. "I kept telling him, 'Greg, this is not a reflection on you, it's a reflection on them.' It's funny, some of these serious fishermen can be the nicest guys in the world, but when a record like this is broken, they are overcome by jealousy," said Walter. "It's breathtaking to see how their character changes. It's, 'Why not me? Why didn't I catch that fish?' I told Greg, 'He who angers you conquers you. I get mad at someone, I'm so angry I can't sleep, so who does the anger hurt?'"

But sometimes Walter wasn't able to obey his own sage advice, and his temper got the best of him. One day he was taking his twelve-year-old grandson Jonathan fishing, and they stopped at a bait shop in Branford on the way. He overheard two fishermen talking loudly about "this asshole who claims he caught the biggest striped bass."

"The intelligent part of me was saying, 'Walter, do not get involved. Keep your mouth shut.' But the emotional part took over, and I went over and said, 'Have you ever met Greg Myerson?' 'No, have you?' And I said, 'Yes, I have. Let me tell you a little bit about him. He was an All-American linebacker. He's six foot four and 270 pounds, with a two-inch fuse. I think he'd be really interested in hearing what you have to say. Would you like to meet him? He could be here in twenty minutes.'"

Everything got very quiet in the shop. Walter paid for his bait and walked outside with his grandson. "Grandpa, I never knew you could be so scary," said Jonathan. "You really scared those men."

Walter had to laugh. "At that point, I had heard so much of this kind of thing, I guess the Marine in me came out," he said.

After they sent in the forms, Greg waited . . . and waited. The world-record approval process took four months. When he got the phone call that his record had been certified, he was in the emergency room of the local hospital, being treated for an infection in his foot where he had been poked by one of the sharp spikes on the back of a striped bass.

THE STRIPED BASS DILEMMA

Greg was right to be concerned about the well-being of the native Atlantic Coast striped bass and the need to protect the large breeders like the world-record bass he had caught. These fish are facing the most dire threats to survival that they've experienced since the late 1970s, when they were nearly driven to extinction.

At that time, the Atlantic States Fisheries Commission seemed unable to take meaningful conservation measures. Established in the early 1940s, the commission is made up of representatives appointed by state governors along the Atlantic Seaboard, with each state having one vote in the decisions they make. Their mandate is to work together to manage the fisheries resource they share and develop quotas for how many fish of each species (based on total tonnage) can be taken without adversely affecting their population. But all too often back then, the parochial interests of each state made it impossible to make compromises and achieve solutions. The states with major commercial fishing interests tended to shoot down any measures that would restrict the amount of striped bass they could harvest. Finally, in 1984, after intense lobbying by conservationists, most of whom were sport fishermen, the U.S. Congress passed the Atlantic Striped Bass Conservation Act, which forced the states to limit the number of bass caught or face a complete shutdown of all commercial and sport fishing of the species. The states complied, establishing a strict moratorium on catching striped bass, and they turned the species' decline around.

By the early 1990s, state game and fish agencies along the Atlantic Seaboard were patting themselves on the back for a job well done, as what looked like the most successful fish management program ever attempted produced a meteoric rise in striped bass numbers, and they opened up the fishery again to both sport and commercial fishing. Many conservationists feel strongly that the harvest numbers were increased prematurely—and their opinion appears to be borne out now as striped bass numbers once again plummet. What makes the situation more ominous than before is that we might not be able to bring them back this time. Striped bass face so many more problems now. They're getting hit from all sides. The bays where they spawn and spend the first couple years of their lives are polluted and becoming increasingly eutrophic from an oversupply of nutrients, which causes explosive growth of algae and other plants and depletes the oxygen. Chesapeake Bay, the greatest striped bass nursery of all, now has vast dead zones caused by agricultural runoff from chicken and pig farms. These oxygen-deprived areas are killing not just crabs and small fish but numerous striped bass as well. The fish can't live in these areas, so they're forced into areas with warmer water, where the heat or a lack of food often kills them.

On top of everything else, the commercial fishing industry is still catching huge numbers of striped bass. In some ways, the harvesting of coastal game fish to sell is an anachronism whose time should be long past. The United States has a long history of exploiting wild animals for profit. In the nineteenth century, commercial hunters in the Northeast decimated deer, moose, and caribou populations to feed lumber camps, which led to the extinction of the caribou in Maine and New Brunswick. In addition, commercial waterfowl hunters up and down the Atlantic Coast went out in rowboats, using punt guns (almost like small cannons), sometimes shooting a hundred or more ducks in a single shot at night as the birds slept on the water. The federal government shut this kind of market hunting down a century ago, declaring that these mammal and bird species are game animals only and cannot be sold. But the coastal game fish were not included in this designation, so commercial harvesting of striped bass and other coastal fish continues in several states.

A persuasive case can certainly be made for declaring the striped bass a noncommercial game fish throughout its historic range on the East Coast. Unlike many commercial fish, which inhabit vast areas of open ocean, the striped bass is a coastal species and has a very limited range, so commercial fishing has a huge impact on them. Fortunately, the species has a large number of devoted allies—most of whom are sport fishermen—who hope to completely shut down the commercial fishing of striped bass.

It's immediately clear as you talk to avid striped bass anglers like Greg how much they admire these fish. Although striped bass are magnificent hunters, they are not viewed as mindless killing machines the way sharks and bluefish often are. There's something unique about a striped bass. Those who know it best say it has "personality." This is exactly what got to Greg: seeing them eye to eye as he hauled them from the water, and feeling a sense of deep sorrow if he harmed them. This experience is what made him turn away from killing striped bass. And he's not the only one. In my travels I've met dozens of people—scientists, conservationists, journalists, and just plain avid fishermen—who are thoroughly dedicated to saving the striped bass.

One such person is Dave Ross, an oceanographer, now retired, who spent the bulk of his career at Woods Hole Oceanographic Institution on Cape Cod. He is the author of numerous scientific and popular articles and several books, most recently *The Fisherman's Ocean*. As a leading oceanographer, he has testified before Congress several times. You don't have to talk with him for long to see how enraptured he is with the beauty and wonder of fish.

"To me, fish are without a doubt the neatest creatures we've got," he said. "They've been around about 450 million years—that's 200 million years longer than the dinosaurs—and they've evolved beautifully with their environment. Their sense of smell is about a million times better than ours. They live in the deepest part of the ocean, the shallowest, the coldest, and the saltiest. They are wonderful."

But he reserves special praise for the striped bass. "A striper has an amazing ability to live in fresh water and salt water. Physiologically, to do that is just startling. And striped bass just seem different from other fish—more curious, more elegant."

Ross has built his life around studying and pursuing striped bass with a rod and reel. "We live on Cape Cod, on the water," he said. "I can basically hop into my boat and go out and fish for a couple of hours. If it's not so good, I come home."

When asked about the status of the striped bass population along the East Coast, he rushes to the defense of the fish. "Think about this: recreational fishermen are allowed to harvest one bass over twenty-eight inches per day," he said. "Most bass over twenty-eight inches— maybe ninety percent—are females. And commercial fishermen are allowed to take a million pounds of fish over thirty-four inches in Massachusetts alone. Those are all breeding-age females. How can a management scheme like that work?"

Fisheries managers talk constantly about biomass—the total tonnage of fish in a fishery—but all too often they don't look at the variety in the size, weight, and age represented in the striped bass population. You need to have the big breeders to have a healthy population. Another problem, according to many sport fishermen I interviewed, is that the fisheries managers reinstituted the striped bass harvest at what's called a maximum sustainable yield (MSY)—a projection based on a rough estimate of the number of fish in the population. These numbers could easily be off by 50 percent or more, and yet the MSY is determined by these estimates.

Ross makes no bones about how wrongheaded fisheries policies are when it comes to the striped bass and the current allowable harvests in most states. "*Harvest* is a phony word," he said. "People have their heads stuck in the sand; they just don't want to acknowledge it. If you look at the statistics for the last ten years, the highs are getting lower and the lows are getting lower. And almost all of the fisheries committees are stacked with commercial fishermen."

From 2006 to 2011, he points out, there was an 83 percent decline in the number of striped bass caught by recreational anglers, so the catch is definitely down. And the data from the National Oceanic and Atmospheric Administration shows that the catch in 2011 was only 16 percent the size of the catch in 2006. He attributes much of this decline to the fact that so many large female bass are being killed off. "It's no surprise that a fifty-pound bass would have more eggs than, say, a ten-pound bass," he said. "But the eggs from those bigger fish are also far more viable. We're harvesting the wrong size of fish and doing it badly. You can't keep harvesting all of the big females. You're killing off the most genetically desirable fish, the ones you need most in the breeding population."

Dean Clark concurs with Ross about the decline in striped bass numbers. Now in his seventies, Clark is a former New York City adman, from the golden age of Madison Avenue in the 1960s. He is a staunch defender of the striped bass. "It's like the 1970s all over again, there's no question about it," he said. "And now, anyone who says, 'Look guys, we're in trouble,' is defined as a tree-hugging Chicken Little, screaming that the sky is falling, and is totally discredited. Well, I'm not a left-wing tree-hugger. I'm a right-wing conservative—but one with a vested interest in conserving the natural world."

In the years-long struggle he and the others have been engaged in to save the striped bass, Clark compares himself to Don Quixote. "It's an uphill battle. All of us are out here tilting at windmills every day. It sometimes feels like a fool's errand in many regards, because the deck is stacked so hard against conservation."

Like a good number of the sport fishermen I interviewed, Clark feels disdainful of the work of some fisheries biologists. "When a biologist says it's a recovered fishery, what do they mean?" he asked. "In the late 1600s in New England, striped bass were so numerous that laws were passed forbidding you from feeding them to slaves and indentured servants more than five days a week."

In those days, Clark points out, people were beach-seining striped bass — going a short distance from shore in a rowboat, encircling the entire school of fish in a long net, and using a team of horses to haul the catch up on shore. And the fish they caught were enormous, with an average size of more than fifty pounds. Now the average size of the striped bass caught by fishermen is less than twenty pounds.

"When you hear the phrase 'a recovered fishery,' and people are chest thumping, take a deep breath, and say, 'Wait a minute: What do you really mean here?'" said Clark. "I remember back in the 1950s when it was very easy for anybody to go out and catch a twenty-five- to fifty-pound bass. Now, experienced fishermen go entire seasons without doing that."

Clark heaps a good deal of the blame on the commercial fishing community and compares it with the market hunters who devastated wild game populations in the late nineteenth and early twentieth centuries. He makes no bones about what he thinks should be done: "When a commercial fisherman turns up at a meeting and says, 'Look, you can't stop me from fishing for striped bass; my livelihood depends on it,' it's the same argument we heard from the market gunners in the 1920s. But back then, the managers had the guts to say: 'I don't care. Go pick up a hammer. Find another job.' Today we have proven methodologies for getting people out of the fishing business in an empathetic way. We can buy them out. It was done thirty years ago with the salmon fishery in Canada."

Like Ross and Clark, many of the anglers working tirelessly on behalf of the striped bass are the same people who fought to save the fish in the 1970s. People like Brad Burns of Maine, who helped push for the 1980s moratorium. Later, in 2003, he was one of the founders of Stripers Forever. At that time, commercial fishermen were pushing for a significantly increased catch quota in Rhode Island, and it looked like it would be approved. The Atlantic States Marine Fisheries Commission, or ASMFC, had already passed a whopping 40 percent increase in the commercial fishing quota, so Burns and the others used it as a rallying cry. The Rhode Island Marine Fisheries Council, which was largely controlled by commercial fishing interests, had already approved the increase, and it needed only to be rubber-stamped by the governor. But Burns and other avid supporters of striped bass conservation stepped in and launched a grassroots campaign aimed at the governor. "We got people to write letters to the governor, attaching cancelled checks from fishing guide services they'd paid for, as well as credit card receipts for gasoline, restaurant meals, and hotels—all to show just how much money sport fishermen were bringing to the state," he said. "The governor finally said, 'This is crazy. We can't do this. I'm getting all these letters from people and copies of checks!'"

A major part of the strategy with groups like Stripers Forever is to show how much sport fishing is adding to the economy. It's a harder sell to make than that of the commercial fishermen who can point to the tonnage of fish they haul in and the amount of money their activities bring to the economy. But revenues from sport fishing are actually significantly higher than those from commercial fishing, and state governments need to be made more aware of this.

Now in his sixties, Burns has never stopped fighting for the striped bass. It's probably safe to say that few people love this fish more than he does. His friend, the late angling author John Cole, wrote that he had once seen Burns kiss a big striped bass on the head before releasing it.

"I enjoy the spectacle of seeing a lot of striped bass—as many big ones as possible," said Burns. "I love seeing them rolling around on the surface of the water, chasing baitfish up on the beach. To me, that's what it's all about—not about taking home a fish to eat." He hasn't killed a striped bass in years. If he doesn't see many stripers when he takes his boat out, he doesn't even try to fish for them. "I'd feel like I was beating up on them," he said. "If there are only a few around, I don't want to be sticking hooks into them. It just doesn't make sense. It ruins it for me."

Burns believes overharvesting is the single biggest issue in the fish's decline. He says commercial striped bass fishing should grind to a halt as soon as possible. "If we don't have enough fish so that some guy can go out and fish all night and keep a fish to take home to his family, we certainly don't have enough to start selling them," he said. "The biggest problem is the commercial fishery's philosophy. You have to have a dead fish to sell it to somebody, so they are all about pushing for more fish." He blames the reduction in the quality of the fishery in Maine to the ratcheting up of the commercial harvest in the 1990s.

"The Kennebec River was a world-class destination in the early 1990s," said Burns. "The number of fish coming into the river was simply mind-boggling. But as soon as they started increasing those commercial fishing quotas south of us, we could see it begin to drop off. And by the early 2000s, it was just a shadow of what it had been.

"You don't need to be a fish scientist to see what's happening to the striped bass," he said. "You can just go out on the water. They are no longer there."

The strategy pursued by Brad Burns and other members of Stripers Forever is to go after the Atlantic Coast states one by one and convince their regulatory agencies to shut down commercial striped bass fishing in their waters. If they get enough of them on board, there will be fewer people representing commercial fishing interests on the Atlantic States Marine Fisheries Commission.

"I want game fish interests to have a majority vote on the commission," said Dean Clark. "Recreational anglers have a far better track record for stewardship of game animals." He wants nothing less than for the striped bass to be the poster child for the near-shore saltwater environment. "That way, we will start managing the resource holistically. We'll look out for the tiny killifish and sand lances and menhaden; the oxygen content of Chesapeake Bay; the PCPs in the Hudson River; because everything that happens to all of those other things will be felt most by the top of the food chain, which is the striped bass. It's going to take a long time. I will not get to see it in my lifetime, but maybe my grandchildren will. If I can help to get us one step closer to a responsible management ethic, based on stewardship as opposed to exploitation, I feel I will have made a contribution."

So far this chapter makes a strong case against the commercial fishing of striped bass, but what about sport fishing? Are recreational anglers without blame? The answer is no. As commercial fishermen proclaim at every opportunity, there are thousands more sport fishermen than commercial fishermen in America, they harvest more striped bass, and the ones they take are often the biggest fish. They have a point. Many people who run guided charter boats after stripers are firmly convinced that unless their sport-fishing clients can slaughter fish and take them home to brag about it, they will not pay money to go fishing. And nothing draws new customers like seeing big striped bass stacked like cordwood on a dock. This should be stopped.

Another thing that needs to end is the emphasis on taking large fish. Why must a striped bass be at least twenty-eight inches in length to be kept, when almost all of the fish that size or larger are already breeders? Why not institute a "slot limit" in which anglers can only keep fish in the twenty- to twenty-seven-inch size range? The salmon fishery on New Brunswick's famed Miramichi River is a prime example of what can be accomplished. The provincial government shut down commercial salmon fishing there in the 1980s, and required recreational anglers to release any salmon larger than twenty-five inches in length; and for the last couple of years, the Miramichi has been a catch-and-release-only fishery. And yet sport anglers still flock there from around the world to take part in the excellent salmon fishing, substantially boosting the local economy.

This approach is common in other segments of sport fishing. Anglers spend a fortune to fly fish for bonefish in the shallow tidal flats of Florida and the Caribbean, and they release all of them. The same with many of the people who pursue native trout: catch-and-release is the order of the day in the best places, and very few fish are killed. Even in the major largemouth bass tournaments taking place in freshwater lakes across the country, the fish are brought in, weighed, and released unharmed. And this is a multimillion-dollar business, with boats, fishing equipment, resorts, and more built around these pursuits. Somehow the striped bass fishery missed the boat. For the good of the striped bass, this needs to change.

Greg hopes to use the notoriety he gained from catching the world-record striped bass to help change people's attitudes toward the killing of big fish. He has been actively promoting catch-and-release striped bass fishing for several years. Most recently, he cosponsored the Fishing Against Cancer Tournament out of Westbrook, Connecticut, in September 2017, which offered major cash prizes in several categories, with all of the profits donated to cancer survivors. And every fish caught had to be released unharmed. As Greg always tells people, "Those fish are far more valuable alive than dead."

ENTREPRENEUR

After 2011, Greg's relationship with competitive fishing became ambivalent at best. He still signed up for the Striper Cup most years, but it was more just to get the T-shirt and pin and to drop in at StriperFest at the end. He was no longer trying to win the tournament. The tournament promoters and press were beside themselves about his attitude and couldn't understand where he was coming from. But to Greg, it just wasn't worth killing big striped bass to win a tournament.

"After killing that fish, something changed in me as a fisherman," said Greg. "I didn't want to kill anything anymore. Even as a deer hunter, I didn't kill as much. I think I grew up as a hunter and fisherman, and it just didn't matter anymore how much I killed or if it was the biggest one. I just wanted to perfect the rattle sinker I was using."

In 2012, the year after he caught his record-breaking striper, Greg decided to try for the striped bass catch-and-release world record, largely to help promote the idea of releasing stripers unharmed. A video crew went out with him to document his effort, so the pressure was on. Miraculously, on that first trip at one o'clock in the morning in the fog, he caught a fifty-three-inch striped bass at Six Mile Reef, while they were filming, and released it successfully. (Catch-and-release striped bass are only measured, not weighed, but it was definitely more than fifty pounds.) Once again he had set a new world record, but this one felt more meaningful. Even though the fish was not as large as his all-tackle world record, he had released it unharmed, and that meant a lot to him.

Along with all the attention Greg received after catching the world-record striped bass, he started getting invited to present paid seminars and speeches at fishing shows. The promoters of these shows also usually offered him booth space for anything he might have to display or sell. He pondered this for a while, wondering what kind of product he might come up with, and then thought, *What about the rattle sinker?* All these years, he'd kept it a tightly held secret, not even telling friends about it, but maybe now was the time to do something with the idea.

Greg and his friends started making the sinkers in his basement. But before launching his business, Greg took his ideas to the University of Connecticut Law School and got their help in registering his patent and trademark, dubbing his invention the RattleSinker. He named his business the World Record Striper Company, and offered his RattleSinkers for sale for the first time in February 2012 at a fishing show in Hartford, Connecticut. They were an instant hit.

"Everyone wanted one," said Greg. "I only made three or four hundred, because I was still making them in my basement, and we sold them all."

For the duration of the three-day fishing show, Greg and his friends would drive home from Hartford and stay up all night assembling and packaging more RattleSinkers to sell, but it was impossible to keep up with the demand.

Greg brought his usual entrepreneurial spirit to the endeavor, the kind he'd exhibited so many times as a child, trapping muskrats, working on farms, and selling bait to fishermen. And he was good at it. He had an incredible capacity for self-promotion and was genuinely enthusiastic about what he was working on. Greg also began designing RattleSinkers for other kinds of fish. He made recordings of crawfish, shrimp, and various crabs and created RattleSinkers that mimicked their sounds as he had done with lobsters. "The RattleSinker can catch a lot more than just striped bass," said Greg. "It can catch any kind of fish."

Two weeks after the Hartford show, Greg was at a fishing show in New Jersey, where they'd invited him to be a speaker, providing him with a lucrative speaker's fee, a sales booth at the show, and a hotel room for him and his crew. Greg's team put together another large production run and quickly sold out again.

"After that, we started adding the rattle sound to flies, floats, and all kinds of different fishing lures," said Greg. "We became known in the industry for our sound-based fishing equipment. The company was cruising along, without any money or advertising behind it, and was growing steadily but not very fast."

Greg started a website for the World Record Striper Company and began selling a significant number of RattleSinkers online. But he still needed another breakthrough to take it to the next level. He needed to get on television somehow.

Greg hadn't really planned to compete in the Striper Cup in 2013. He had registered, like he always does, but was releasing all the fish he caught. Then one day when he was fishing with his cousin Michael, he hooked into a huge striped bass. The conditions at sea that day were brutal, with high winds and whitecaps. Other anglers around them quickly pulled up their lines and moved their boats to give him room to fight the striper. A short time later, after an epic battle, he landed the fish, and it was spectacular, a seventy-three-pounder. Even though he knew it was a tournament-winning fish, he planned to release it instead of taking it in to be weighed and registered for the Striper Cup, but unfortunately it had died in the fight.

"There was no releasing it," said Greg. "It wasn't even moving. I don't know what happened. It must have had a heart attack or something. I even tried releasing it in the water, but it floated. It was done. I would've let it go otherwise."

With that fish, Greg suddenly had the biggest striped bass caught in the 2013 Striper Cup, so he went ahead and registered it. But the story didn't end there. Later that evening, as always, Greg continued fishing, and he hooked the biggest striped bass he's ever seen—a fish so powerful it pulled the boat forward against the strong current of a surging tide, peeling more than 200 yards of line from his reel before he could turn it around and work it slowly back to the boat.

"Oh my God," said Michael as the fish came into view. "It's way bigger than your world record."

They finally hauled the bass into the boat and tried to weigh it. Although the scale went up to ninety pounds, the enormous weight of the fish completely bottomed it out. They hurriedly measured the length and girth of the fish and took some pictures, but it was so huge, Michael couldn't even get far enough back in the boat to include the fish's head and tail in one photograph. (Using a standard formula for calculating a striped bass's weight from its length and girth measurements, the fish weighed approximately 106 pounds.)

Then came the moment of truth. Greg had not brought his official International Game Fish Association measuring device, which you must use if a fish is to qualify for an IGFA catch-and-release world record. (He had left it in his own boat, and Michael didn't have one.) He knew that if he released the fish, it would not count toward any record. But if he killed it and brought it to the dock to be officially weighed and measured, he would set an all-tackle world record that might well stand for decades. What was he to do?

He didn't hesitate. As Michael stood awestruck, Greg started to haul the fish back over the side of the boat.

"What are you going to do?" Michael asked, aghast, as the fish went into the water.

Greg didn't say anything. He gently held the fish by its lower jaw as the water flowed through its gills, fully reviving it. "I could see her eye, big as a silver dollar, rolling around and looking at me," said Greg. "The fish was beautiful. She didn't have a mark on her." He looked at the great fish for a few seconds more, then released his grip.

"She had her mouth clamped down on my thumb, and that was the only thing holding her. She was free to go, but she just held on, looking at me. And then, *whoosh!* She took off and was gone, and that was that."

Greg stared off wistfully as he told me the story. "It wasn't worth it to me to kill the fish just to get another piece of paper to hang on my wall."

After watching the massive striped bass swim away, Greg's cousin lit up a cigarette, inhaled deeply, and released a huge cloud of smoke. "Shit, what just happened?" said Michael. "No one's going to believe this."

You might well ask, how does Greg Myerson address the paradox of wanting to protect the large breeders in the striped bass population and yet potentially giving thousands of anglers the keys to the kingdom when it comes to catching the biggest stripers? After all, no one can force the people who use his RattleSinker to release their fish. It's a fair question, and one that Greg does not shy away from. In all of his interactions with other anglers, he stresses the importance of releasing the large stripers they catch—in his conversations, his talks, and in his interviews with the media.

"I'm trying to get the message out about how stupid it is to kill these fish," said Greg. "Why do it? To take a picture? It's just not worth it. I always encourage the charter customers I take out fishing to release their fish. And I set an example by never keeping the stripers I catch."

SO YOU WANT TO
BE A TV STAR?

"**W**hat's this *Shark Tank* stuff?" asked Greg's friend Mike as he picked up an envelope from the top of a stack of letters on Greg's kitchen table. "Mind if I open it?"

Greg shrugged. Mike tore the envelope open and dumped out its contents: a cover letter and an application to become a contestant on *Shark Tank*, a popular reality show produced by Sony Pictures and appearing on ABC. Each week, various entrepreneurs appear on the show and pitch their get-rich-quick schemes to a panel of billionaires—the Sharks—in an attempt to get them to invest in their businesses.

"You should fill this out," said Mike. "It'd be amazing if you got on *Shark Tank*. Think of all the RattleSinker orders you'd get."

"I don't know," said Greg. "I just want to go fishing." The two had just finished loading up Greg's pickup truck with their rods and reels and planned to spend the evening fishing for striped bass in Long Island Sound. As always, Greg was eager to get out on the water and didn't want to waste time filling out paperwork.

"This'll only take a few minutes," said Mike. "I'll just read the questions to you and write down your answers."

Greg didn't know much about the show and didn't care about becoming a contestant. A few weeks earlier Gail, a friend of Greg's who was working with him when he launched the World Record Striper Company, had contacted *Shark Tank* through its website and requested an application for him. It had just arrived that day.

As soon as Mike finished filling out the application, he put it in an envelope. He dropped it off at the post office on the way to the boat dock. And then nothing happened—for nearly three years.

Greg was working as an electrician for the Connecticut Department of Transportation, and one wintry day in the middle of February, while he was directing traffic for another electrician who was up on a cherry picker, repairing a highway streetlight, he heard the sound of an email arriving on his iPhone. A quick read told him it was a talent scout from *Shark Tank* asking Greg to call her and answer a few questions about the business venture he wanted to pitch on the show. Intrigued, he put some orange cones in the intersection and climbed into the DOT truck to make the call. It soon became obvious she knew nothing about his business, so Greg gave her a quick description of the RattleSinker and the World Record Striper Company, and she went through his website as they talked.

"If we're interested, you'll hear back from us soon," she told him.

"Yeah, yeah, whatever," said Greg.

"No, really," she said. "And you know, you should be very glad you got this call. Only one person in thirty thousand gets this far."

By the time Greg got home that night, he'd already received another email from *Shark Tank*, this time from two producers, Alan and Michael, who wanted to talk to him. He called the number and they spoke with him briefly, inviting him to send them some video footage so they could evaluate Greg's on-camera presence. He wondered what he could do. Then he thought, *I could tell them, "The most important thing a fisherman needs to know is the right kind of bait to use to attract the kind of fish you're after. If I'm fishing for sharks, I'd use something like this"—and then cast a big wad of money right at the camcorder.* Vinny came over and they worked on it together, then put the completed video on a DVD and sent it to the producers. It wasn't great, but Greg figured it should give them an idea of his pitch.

But then it was hurry-up-and-wait again. Three months went by, and Greg still hadn't heard anything more from them. By then another television production company had approached him about creating a fishing reality show. The producers already had a successful classic car show on the A&E cable network and were pushing hard to get Greg on board. Three of them showed up at his house, contract in hand, driving three separate sports cars, and Greg was planning to sign it. *Why not?* he figured. *Nothing else is going on, and it sounds like a great opportunity.* He'd pretty much given up on *Shark Tank*. The only problem was, once he signed the contract, there was no going back; you can be on only one reality show. The contract would put an end to any hopes of ever going on *Shark Tank*. And the thought of going on *Shark Tank* was particularly appealing to him. Not only would his product get a lot of great exposure on the show, he might be able to get one of the Sharks to give him the financial backing he needed to take the RattleSinker to the next level.

Greg sat on his couch in the living room, pen in hand, and was just about to sign the contract when a friend came over. He set the pen down and introduced her to the producers. She was amazed when she heard about the show and wanted to hear all about Greg's part in it. Half an hour went by before Greg finally picked up the pen again. Just as he was about to sign, his iPhone lit up. He set the pen down and checked his phone. He had a new email—from the *Shark Tank* producers. They told him they loved his video and wanted to talk to him about possibly appearing on the show.

"Sorry, I can't sign your contract," said Greg. "I'm going to be on *Shark Tank*."

This was a bit of an exaggeration. *Shark Tank* contestants can be dropped at any stage along the way as they go through various interviews and tryouts. Even after traveling to Los Angeles and making a pitch to the Sharks, a contestant still might not end up on the show if their segment isn't interesting enough. And Greg was a very long way from even being invited to the studio for a tryout.

Two of the men were furious and stormed out of his apartment, but one of them wished him well and said he hoped they might work together sometime. Perhaps it was a rash decision on Greg's part. Here he had a TV show in the bag, albeit one that was less well-known than *Shark Tank*. And he still had endless hoops to jump through before he would know whether he would really be on the show. Many—perhaps most—people who make it this far still don't get on *Shark Tank*; it's incredibly competitive, with very few available spots.

Each Monday at 4:00 p.m., Greg would have a conference call with producers Alan and Michael (familiarity soon made them Al and Mike) and go through dry runs of his *Shark Tank* pitch, delivering it again and again and again. This went on for a couple of months, until he was nearly completely burned out on the whole thing. But by then, Al and Mike felt he was their boy, and they really wanted him to be on the show. They started sending paperwork, sometimes fifty pages at a time, for him to sign. Fortunately, Greg had a friend who offered to help. She would go through all the papers in a single night and have them ready for him to sign and return the next morning. Eventually it all came together, and they asked him to ship RattleSinkers, displays, signage, and other promotional materials he would need for the show to Sony Pictures. "We're bringing you to L.A.," they told him. "Your plane tickets are in the mail."

Greg wasn't supposed to discuss his possible appearance on *Shark Tank* with anyone, but he couldn't resist letting his brother Dave and his college roommate Bear Judkins know. Besides, he would need their help to make it happen. Greg was terrified of flying—ever since he'd been on an airliner that nearly crashed during an electrical storm while traveling from Florida to Vermont on New Year's Eve 1999. Over Atlanta, the plane had suddenly plunged several thousand feet, finally pulling out just seconds before it would have hit the ground. Greg swore he would never fly again, and so far he'd kept his promise. But now he had to get to Los Angeles, and the studio had sent him plane tickets.

Bear drove to Wallingford to see him. "You look like shit, Greg," he told him. "But don't worry. I'll fly with you. Everything will be fine."

Greg was a basket of anxiety in the days leading up to his trip and was eating Xanax like candy. He also had a major flare-up of ulcerative colitis, which had plagued him for several years, and was taking prednisone to control the inflammation and bleeding. He was nearly comatose on the flight west.

As soon as they stepped out of the security area at LAX, Greg and Bear spotted a man holding up a sign reading "Greg Myerson." They followed him outside to a *Shark Tank* van that was waiting at the curbside. They were taken to a hotel in Culver City, where all of the aspiring *Shark Tank* contestants—perhaps fifteen in all—were staying. The show's security staff kept a close eye on everyone. No one was allowed to discuss their products and pitches with each other, which made conversation difficult. All of them had arrived on Thursday, and the following morning they were taken in two separate vans to the Sony Pictures studio to begin the auditions.

The area of the studio they went to looked just like the *Shark Tank* set, but the "Sharks" weren't there—only photographs of them propped up on a table. The room was full of people—producers, lawyers, web developers—sitting at tables, hunched over their laptop computers, staring intently at the potential contestants as they presented their sales pitches. It was enough to make anyone nervous. Greg peeked in on them during some of the other pitches. The producers sat stone-faced and silent through most of them—until they got to Greg. As soon as Greg swung his toy fishing rod forward, flipping a wad of dollar bills right to the center of the head producer's laptop, they all burst out laughing, and at the end of his pitch everyone stood up and applauded. They sent him back to his hotel room as soon as he was finished and said they'd let him know soon, one way or another, whether he was going to be on the show. He didn't hear anything more until that night, when the producer called and said Greg was moving to the next step and would be making his pitch to the Sharks on Tuesday. "So just enjoy your weekend and be ready to go at nine o'clock on Tuesday morning," he said.

This was the worst possible setup for Greg. He can be amazingly relaxed if he has to talk spontaneously at any kind of event or even on television or radio. He's a natural performer. But if he has to spend hours — or in this case days — in anticipation, worrying about how something like this will turn out, it eats him up inside. Plus everything about *Shark Tank* is intentionally ominous and menacing. Even the opening credits are scary — tall skyscrapers viewed from below with silhouettes of hammerhead sharks swirling around above (with a nice shark bite out of the letter K in *Tank*) while music reminiscent of the theme from *Jaws* plays in the background. And the first things the contestants see when they enter the *Shark Tank* set are the stern faces of the Sharks peering intently at them, like predators viewing their next meal.

The Sharks are a panel of potential investors who consider offers from aspiring entrepreneurs hoping to get someone to grubstake their product, invention, or business. The show seeks to capture "the drama of pitch meetings and the interaction between the entrepreneurs and tycoons." *Shark Tank* plays up the tension to the hilt. It can be a humiliating experience for contestants, many of whom are teased and ridiculed by the Sharks. (The show actually requires each contestant to talk to a company psychiatrist before they leave the studio, to make sure they're okay.) Greg was worried — it was one thing to go home empty-handed, but what if he disgraced himself in front of a national viewing audience, including virtually everyone he'd ever known?

As soon as he heard from the producer, Greg telephoned his brother to let him know what was going on. Dave lives in Portland, Oregon, but he had come to Los Angeles to help Greg prepare for *Shark Tank*. He had already been helping him with his RattleSinker business and knew all the details. Dave told me he views himself as Greg's consigliere, helping him make decisions, evaluating the different options he has to choose from.

Dave was staying at another hotel near the airport. "I'd drive there in the morning, have a cup of coffee with him, and put him on the van," he said. "Then I'd go somewhere and wait for him to call, to find out if he made it through the day okay. I'd go back up to his room at night and grill him: 'What are you going to say if they say this?' 'What are you going to say if they say that?' It was almost like a presidential debate prep. I think it helped, but he got so pissed off at me."

"After a while, I'm not listening to a thing he's saying," said Greg. "I'm just sitting there, and I'm like, 'yeah, yeah, yeah.'"

Eventually Dave came to realize they'd reached a point of diminishing returns and that this intense drilling was just making Greg more stressed, so he changed tactics. "You know, Greg, you got this far just doing this goofy shit, so you might as well just keep doing it," Dave told him. "The thing is, you're a fisherman, not a businessman; just be yourself and don't worry about any of the commercial aspects or anything. These guys are going to see a business opportunity or not. If they don't, you know what you're doing tomorrow. So let's just hang around L.A. this weekend and have a good time."

They drove to Venice Beach and walked around enjoying the warm California sun, and even went fishing at a nearby pier. Greg could feel the stress melting away. But it came back with a vengeance on Monday night, and he barely slept at all. He couldn't eat any breakfast the next morning as he got ready for his day at the studio. Dave was standing with him when Greg boarded the *Shark Tank* van. He stood at attention and snapped a military salute at Greg as it drove away.

Although he arrived at the studio before 9:00 a.m., Greg spent most of the day in his dressing room. It was a torturous experience. "I had no idea when it would be my turn," said Greg. "I just sat there eating prednisone and Xanax to keep myself from freaking out." The producers, Al and Mike, kept coming into Greg's dressing room and asking him to go through his pitch again. He was so exhausted—and so sick of giving the pitch—he kept screwing it up. They were both aghast.

"Look, I know I'll do fine when I'm in there," Greg told them. "Just leave me alone. I promise you I will not fuck up under pressure." The two glanced at each other, a look of terror in their eyes.

"I don't know what they were thinking at that point," said Greg. "They were like, 'Oh my God!'" But they left him alone.

He finally got the call at 6:00 p.m. telling him he was up next. He'd been alone in his dressing room since Al and Mike had left him that morning. "I was one of the last people to go," said Greg. "They came to my dressing room and picked me up in a golf cart." It was a scorching day, nearly 110 degrees Fahrenheit as he stepped out of his air-conditioned dressing room. They drove him to a huge studio building that resembled an airplane hangar. A production person met him at the door.

"We're going to bring you in, mike you up, and make sure all your stuff is set up the way you want it," he told Greg. He followed the man inside to the *Shark Tank* set. A false wall that could be wheeled out had a mount of Greg's world-record striped bass and certificates for each of his records, but they were covered by a tan nylon shroud attached to a fishing rod, so he could twitch it away and unveil them at the appropriate moment. A wooden table stood in front with displays of Greg's RattleSinkers. To the right was a rack with several fishing rods and reels, and to the left, a sign with his World Record Striper Company logo in black on a white background.

The Sharks were already sitting in there, but they didn't pay attention to Greg. They were all looking at their iPhones, checking emails or sending tweets. The Sharks included Mark Cuban, a billionaire tech mogul and owner of the famed Dallas Mavericks basketball team; Lori Greiner, who holds over 100 patents and has launched some 400 products, grossing more than a billion dollars in sales; Daymond John, a branding expert behind multiple global brands, generating billions in sales; Kevin O'Leary, a shrewd venture capitalist nicknamed

"Mr. Wonderful," who made his fortune selling a children's educational company for more than four billion dollars; and Robert Herjavec, who founded one of the world's preeminent cyber security firms. Greg felt a chill when he saw them and looked away.

He told the man that everything in his display looked great. After he was miked up, they took him to a waiting room where he sat on a couch for another small eternity. He knew he had to overcome his fears to avoid making a fool of himself. "Don't be such a fucking pussy!" he shouted at himself. "They're just people. Get your fucking self together, man!" Then he slapped himself hard in the face.

The production man finally came back and told Greg he needed to take him to the entrance passage, where two huge doors are opened to let contestants enter the *Shark Tank* set.

"So, you're getting yourself psyched up, huh?" the man asked.

"What do you mean?" said Greg.

"We heard everything you were saying through your mike," he said, laughing. Greg blanched. "Don't worry about it. You'd be surprised at all the shit I hear."

Although on the show the two heavy doors appear to open automatically, actually two men in hardhats open them manually. Greg nodded at them as he stood waiting.

"Are you union guys?" he asked. They both nodded.

"Me, too," he said. "I'm a union electrician." They both fist-bumped with Greg.

"Go in there and kill it, man," one of them said.

"I definitely will," said Greg.

INTO THE SHARK TANK

As Greg stood there, waiting to make his entrance, a loudspeaker blared: "Next into the Tank is an entrepreneur who hopes to lure the Sharks with a big fish." With that, the doors swung open and Greg strode onto the set, stopping at his mark on the floor. He looked every inch the fisherman, clad in a light blue nylon fishing shirt, tan pants, boat shoes, and a World Record Striper Company cap.

The first half-minute or so of a *Shark Tank* segment is always an intense stare-off between the contestant and the Sharks—some smirking, others glaring menacingly. And it's only the beginning of what can be an excruciating experience for a contestant, far more stressful than it might appear to a television audience, because the final version of each segment is much shorter than the original taping. In Greg's case, for example, the televised segment only lasts about seven minutes, but he actually spent close to an hour in the studio making his pitch to the Sharks. But Greg was absolutely ready. In the initial stare-off, he instantly locked eyes with Kevin O'Leary and maintained his gaze until O'Leary finally looked away. At that moment, Greg was in his element. Although he still had a raging fever and intense pain from his colitis flare-up, he barely noticed it. A sense of intense calm came over him and all of his fears vanished.

"Hello, Sharks," he said. "My name is Greg Myerson from Wallingford, Connecticut. My company is the World Record Striper Company, and I'm seeking $75,000 in exchange for 20 percent of my company." He felt completely relaxed and confident for the first time in weeks.

"Sharks, I'm a fisherman . . . a darn good one, because I know to catch big fish you have to use the right bait."

Mark Cuban smiled broadly, obviously enjoying Greg's pitch.

"So, if I'm fishing for a shark, I'm probably going to use something like this." Greg reached behind the false wall of his display and pulled out his daughter's pink Barbie fishing rod with a thick wad of cash tied to the end of the line. With a flick of his wrist, he cast it at Kevin O'Leary, sitting thirty feet away, landing it right in his lap. Everyone went *Ohhh!* in amazement.

"I figured you could use some cash," said Greg.

O'Leary smirked disdainfully at the wad, which contained only one-dollar bills, and tossed it back. Greg ignored him and went on with his pitch. "When I'm fishing, I use my very own product: the Greg Myerson RattleSinker." He then explained how his product attracted big fish by mimicking the sounds of their favorite prey. "You hear that?" he said as he vigorously shook the sinker. "To fish, that's the sound of the dinner bell ringing." He said the RattleSinker had made him one of the most famous fishermen in the world, and then he picked up a fishing rod that was attached to the tan-colored shroud on the wall behind him and pulled it down, revealing the mount of his world-record striped bass. It was spectacular.

"You caught that?" said Cuban, amazed. "That could knock over your boat."

"Yes, I did." Greg told them the striped bass world record was the most sought-after saltwater fishing record in America and that it had stood for twenty-nine years before he shattered it. He pointed at the framed world-record certificate from the International Game Fish Association. He said it took about an hour for him to reel in the fish. "I hope it doesn't take me that long to net a deal with you."

Greg pulled out a flat display container of RattleSinkers and walked over to the Sharks, letting each of them take one out and examine it. They all started shaking them. Daymond John asked Greg if he caught the fish using a RattleSinker.

"Yes, I did. And I've caught three other world records with this product." When the Sharks asked why the striped bass world record was so sought after, Greg told them the striped bass was "America's fish." Anyone can fish for it, without a yacht or expensive equipment. "You can fish from shore," he said. Lori Greiner nodded enthusiastically and said how popular the striped bass is at Martha's Vineyard, where she goes every summer. But she wondered why the RattleSinker is so effective at catching big fish.

"It's a good question," said Greg, and then he gave a rambling reply that didn't exactly answer her question but was entertaining. "I've been a fisherman my whole life. I started fishing at age two in a sewer and . . . probably a good thing I never caught anything there." Daymond John looked skeptical as Greg spoke. "But at eight I made a fly out of my grandmother's parrot . . . and I hated that thing. It would attack me." Mark Cuban and a couple of other sharks laughed. "When it died, she said, 'Would you bury it for me?' And I said, 'Yeah, yeah, yeah.' I tied twelve flies out of it. I caught a trout. It got me on the front page of the town newspaper."

"Oh, you are the man," said Cuban, laughing while Kevin O'Leary looked dead serious.

"When I came up with this product, I knew that these fish are sound-driven. They hunt through sound and vibration first. They're also nearsighted."

O'Leary shook the sinker near his ear, with the same stern expression on his face. Cuban inquired why, if this product is so good, no one else had thought of it before.

"Nobody's as smart as me," said Greg.

Cuban laughed. "I like your humble humble-brag," he said.

The Sharks soon got down to business, bombarding Greg with questions about how he developed the RattleSinker, how and where he was selling them, how many he had sold, and how much profit he made from each one. He admitted he'd only sold about seven thousand so far. They looked incredulous. Greg told them he'd been selling RattleSinkers only since he broke the world record, but they had been his secret weapon for years. He'd earned about $55,000 so far selling them.

"So you're not the smartest guy in the world," said Cuban.

Greg shrugged. "I'm not a great businessman, but I'm a great fisherman."

"That's pretty obvious," said Cuban.

He said Greg was not really an entrepreneur but a "wantrepreneur" and still trying to figure out what he was doing.

Greg took the teasing from the Sharks in stride and had no qualms about going on the counterattack, giving as good—or better—than what they threw at him. He had one of his best exchanges with Daymond John. The producers, Mike and Al, had told Greg that Daymond John was an avid fisherman, and they had a picture of him holding up a pathetically small fish he had caught. They said if a moment came up in the taping where Greg could mention the photo, they would put it up on the screen and get a laugh. The opportunity came about three-quarters of the way through the taping when John said, "Let a fellow fisherman tell you, you better take this," and Greg pounced. "Yeah, I know you're a fisherman," he said. "I've seen a picture of a fish you recently caught." And the image popped up on the big screen.

"Come on, man!" Greg teased. "That thing isn't even big enough to be my bait!" All of the Sharks except Daymond John burst out laughing. John pointed out it was big enough for a sandwich. "Not for any of the sandwiches I eat," said Greg.

Another funny moment came when Greg mentioned a new film that would be coming out soon titled *Running the Coast*, produced by

Jamie Howard of Howard Films, about East Coast anglers' obsession with striped bass. Naturally, Greg figured prominently in the film, and Cuban teased him about it, calling him a movie star.

"He asked me who was going to play me in the movie," Greg told me. "'Brad Pitt!' I said. 'Who else would play me? But who's going to play you, Mark?' The Sharks started throwing out names of actors, and they were all ugly. All of them were laughing and teasing each other."

At one point near the end of the taping, Robert Herjavec decided to drop out of the bidding for the RattleSinker, saying, "I'll make this real easy. I'm out."

"Then you're dead to me," said Greg, and he wouldn't even look at Herjavec anymore. "I held up my hand and blocked him out of my view," he said later. "I would just look at the other four. They were all laughing. They loved it."

Greg thrived on the back-and-forth banter. Unfortunately, these and several other of his favorite moments in his pitch failed to make the final cut and did not appear on *Shark Tank*. But what did appear was great and gave his budding company a huge boost. Greg's segment built quickly to a climax after Mark Cuban put an offer on the table.

"I'm going to simplify things," said Cuban. "I invested in a company named Shell Bobber, and I'm going to make you exactly the same offer I made to them: $80,000 for 33 percent."

Greg thought the offer sounded good, but he was curious if any of the other Sharks had counteroffers. Robert Herjavec, Lori Greiner, and Daymond John had quickly dropped out, leaving only Mark Cuban and Kevin O'Leary in contention for a share in Greg's company. O'Leary implied that he could do better for him, but Cuban cut him off before he could spell out his offer.

"We all know what Kevin . . . the kind of offers he makes, right?" said Cuban. "So I'm going to put you on the spot. If you want to listen to Kevin, that's fine. I'm out." The camera zoomed in on Greg as he grimaced. "If you don't want to listen to Kevin and take my offer . . ."

"Well, that's interesting," O'Leary interjected. "Because my offer might be much better."

Then the Sharks raised the tension to the boiling point, talking rapidly over each other, building up to a stressful cacophony as the camera swirled around them: "Make up your mind!" "You've got to de-cide!" "You better take this offer!" "The money is on the table!" "What are you going to do?"

"*Dun-dun-dun-dun*," Robert Herjavec mimicked the sound that plays whenever the great white shark is about to appear in *Jaws*. Mark Cuban smiled. They all stared hard at Greg, and he stared right back.

After a long, intense pause: "Mark, I'll take the deal," said Greg.

"You got it," said Cuban, getting up from his chair and walking to Greg.

"Thank you, man," Greg said as they shook hands. Then they hugged. "One world champ to another," Greg added.

"Absolutely, man. We'll have fun with it."

As soon as Greg walked back through the double doors, Al and Mike jumped on him. "They were all pumped up," said Greg. "They came running in and jumped up. They're both tiny guys, and I actu-ally caught one of them." They took him to see the psychiatrist who decompresses everyone who appears on the show. She asked Greg if he felt humiliated. "Fuck no!" he told her. "I just got a deal with Mark Cuban."

THE PENDULUM SWINGS

As I sped through the second red light, I glanced over at Greg, riding in the passenger seat, his head leaning against the side window. Although it was late in the evening and dark, the streetlights at the intersection lit up the inside of my truck, and for an instant I could see how pale he looked. He was barely conscious. *I should've called a damn ambulance,* I cursed under my breath, then looked away and drove faster, desperately racing to Yale–New Haven Hospital, still nearly ten miles away.

I felt so stupid. I should have brought him there two or three hours earlier, when we first gave up our plans to spend all night fishing on Long Island Sound. We both knew the fishing would be great that night, with numerous huge stripers passing through off Block Island, where we planned to go. I should have realized that Greg would have had to be on death's door to pass up the chance to go out and catch some of them. He'd had a major flare-up of ulcerative colitis, which had plagued him on and off for several years, and had been self-medicating with the powerful steroid prednisone for a couple of weeks, to treat severe inflammation and internal bleeding. It had always worked for him in the past, but somehow this time was different. He was only getting sicker. On the drive back from Westbrook Harbor, we'd had to stop at a gas station so Greg could use the restroom, and he had nearly filled the toilet bowl with blood. When we finally got to his house, I asked him if he needed to go to the emergency room.

"No, I just need to get some rest," Greg told me. "Let's just wait until morning. If I'm still in bad shape, I'll go to the hospital."

"Are you sure?" I asked. He nodded and walked to his bedroom. "Okay," I said, as I started unrolling my sleeping bag on the couch in his living room. But I didn't feel good about it. Greg looked terrible. He had been sweating profusely and shivering, obviously burning up with fever and in a lot of pain. Awful thoughts kept nagging at me: *What if he doesn't make it until morning? What if he bleeds to death as I'm dithering around, trying to figure out what to do? Maybe I should call an ambulance.* I was filled with indecision. I finally couldn't take it any longer. I went into Greg's room, where he lay sprawled across the bed with his clothes still on, and told him, "Get in the car. We're going to the hospital."

A minute later, we were on our way, speeding to New Haven, nearly fifteen miles away. But had we waited too long? It seemed obvious to me now that Greg was in imminent danger of dying. Why hadn't I done something sooner? He was bleeding out inside and only a hospital could help him, if I could just get him there in time.

As we finally pulled in at the emergency room door, I parked illegally along the curb and ran inside looking for someone to help him. By then, Greg could barely walk. I must have looked terror-stricken as I babbled on about my friend who was bleeding to death in my car outside. An emergency room staffer quickly brought out a wheelchair and whisked Greg away to see a doctor, while the other patients ahead of us still sat in the waiting room.

I stayed at the hospital for a good part of the night as the medical staff gave Greg a blood transfusion and stabilized him. A couple of hours later, Greg seemed much improved. The transfusion and the pain medication had done wonders. The color had returned to his face and he was sitting up in bed, but he still seemed very weak. Now that the life-and-death situation had passed—or at least been put on hold—the doctor took the opportunity to let Greg know how appalled he was that he had waited so long to be treated. He should have come in at least two or three weeks earlier, he grumbled, and it was truly amazing he had survived at all. Greg nodded and looked away. Then a nurse standing nearby, who kept peering intently at Greg, said he looked very familiar. Greg mentioned he'd been on *Shark Tank* recently, and the nurse's and doctor's faces instantly lit up. "I saw you on that show!" said the doctor, gleefully. "The fisherman!" And suddenly the old Greg was back, his face beaming as he started spinning hilarious yarns about *Shark Tank* and his bantering with Mark Cuban and the others. He had everyone in the room laughing, including a couple more nurses who had heard the laughter and come to investigate. Once again, he was in his element with an audience of eager listeners. I knew right then that he was on the road to recovery and it was safe to leave.

I excused myself and told Greg I'd be back in the morning. As I walked through the hospital corridors, trying to find my way out, I could still hear peals of laughter coming from Greg's room. Thankfully, my truck had not been towed away, so I climbed inside and drove back to Greg's house in the darkness.

The next morning when I came to visit him, Greg said that the doctor had told him he was sure he would not have lived until morning if he had not come to the emergency room the night before. "You know, you saved my life," he told me, then smiled. "I don't know how many more lives I've got left; I'm definitely way past nine lives." We both laughed. I was so relieved that everything had worked out. For a while, during the last few miles before we got to the hospital, his survival seemed anything but certain to me.

I left for home the following day. The doctors kept Greg in the hospital for ten days before they dared to release him, no doubt fearing he might have a sudden relapse of the dangerous bleeding and wanting to monitor him closely as they worked to stabilize his condition. His internal swelling was so bad that the hospital couldn't perform a colonoscopy to see exactly what was going on. But they were trying a different medication, which seemed to be improving his condition.

As I drove home to Central New York, I thought about Greg's life and what a wild ride he'd had. I know that everyone's life is like a pendulum, with numerous highs and lows between the cradle and the grave. But with Greg, the swings of the pendulum are so much more extreme than with anyone else I know, casting him from the lofty heights of his *Shark Tank* appearance, when he won over the hard-nosed Sharks as well as a national television audience, to this near-death experience a few months later. Of course, the seeds of this downturn were actually sown during the run-up to his *Shark Tank* appearance, when his stress level went through the roof for weeks as he pondered the possibility that he might make a fool of himself on national television, and he was also terrified about flying to Los Angeles and back. His colitis had returned with a vengeance at that time and never really abated. But I felt strongly that Greg's pendulum would soon swing upward again to heights he'd never yet seen. It didn't take long.

A short time after he recovered, Greg met Mark Freedman at a charity fishing tournament in New York City. Freedman was very taken with Greg's charisma and fascinating backstory. "I thought, *This guy is so colorful, he deserves a shot at doing some kind of TV show,*" he told me — and Freedman is just the person who could make that happen. As a film and television producer and licensing agent (and founder and president of Surge Licensing), he is a star-maker of the first magnitude. It was Freedman who "discovered" a little-known cult comic book called *Teenage Mutant Ninja Turtles* and turned it into a billion-dollar franchise, spinning off popular movies, television shows, live events, video games, and various merchandise. He has also produced outdoor television programs, most notably *The Best and Worst of Tred Barta*, which ran for nearly a decade on cable television — and featured another charismatic, one-of-a-kind outdoorsman.

Freedman has been brainstorming with Bob Wheeler (of Wheeler

Communications)—the producer/director he teamed up with on Tred Barta's show—to develop a concept for a reality television show featuring Greg. Most fishing shows currently on cable television are "time buys"—that is, the producers buy a particular time slot from a cable network and have to fund it themselves or through a large advertiser. The shows often end up being essentially a thirty-minute advertisement for a product or company. But Freedman and Wheeler have much larger ambitions for this project. They want to create an original series—in which case the television network or streaming service would pay for the show. And they want it to be much more than just a fishing show.

"I don't want to have what I call a 'bent rod' show, catching big fish on every episode," said Freedman. "There are just so many times you can shout *Ooh!* and *Ah!* and *Wow!* It gets boring really fast. I'm looking to broaden this out and have it appeal to a general audience—attracting the outdoor fisherman and hunter but also drawing in people from other walks of life, who'll say, 'Wow, this is cool. I really like this guy and the people he surrounds himself with.'"

Freedman and Wheeler got a taste of what this show could be last May when they dropped in on Greg and his crew at the World Record Striper Company headquarters—Greg's basement—and spent a couple of days doing preliminary filming. (Wheeler had come all the way from Atlanta.) They took a shotgun approach—no plans, no script, just shooting tons of video of whatever took place. Several of Greg's friends were there—Matt, who was with him when he caught the world-record striper; Bill, an old friend from his high school football team who had lived with him in the condo at Lake Tahoe; Jeff, the captain of the World Record Striper Company charter boat; another Jeff who often crews on the boat; and a guy everyone called The Vegetable, whom Greg had known since his Little League days. The Vegetable, or "Veggie" for short, bears a striking resemblance to Kramer on the TV show *Seinfeld,* with a shock of wild, blown-back hair and a manic quality that brings a jolt of high energy to the shop—energy that unfortunately doesn't seem to transfer into productivity. Everyone sat in folding chairs at an old poker table—the same table Herb and his mob associates had sat around some forty years earlier.

They were ostensibly filling orders, bagging up RattleSinkers, putting them in Priority Mail boxes, and sending them to people who had bought them through the company website. But there was constant laughter, bickering, teasing, and food breaks—the infectious chaos of Greg's day-to-day existence—so very little work was accomplished. It started out when Bill brought a kosher breakfast of lox and bagels for everyone, and they spent an hour munching on the food, talking, and laughing.

Freedman and Wheeler stepped outside briefly to talk privately but were overheard. "Every time I've been here it's like this," said Freedman, laughing. "This is the way these guys really are. None of this is staged. This is the way the company runs. It's great!" Wheeler nodded enthusiastically and laughed.

A short time later, Ralph D'Arco of Radfish Lures, who is working with Greg on a new line of freshwater jigs for catching largemouth bass, showed up. He had driven down from Springfield, Massachusetts, and brought the crew a bunch of Italian food—calzones, sausage, meatballs, and even cannolis—so they started scarfing it down instead of working. And then Greg's girlfriend, Mary, a fitness trainer, walked in just as he was filling his face. She exploded. "What are you doing?" she said angrily. "We were supposed to go walking." She had been urging him to lose weight and get in better shape. "If you're not going to take this seriously then I'm not going to waste my time!" Wheeler just kept right on shooting video through their whole exchange. And when the two of them finally left to take their walk, he went along and filmed it. Mary was as good on camera as Greg was, and the chemistry between them was electrifying.

Later that afternoon, Greg went out fishing, taking Freedman and Wheeler and a few other people, even though a howling gale was whipping across the water. It was hopeless to try to go out into Long Island

Sound, but Greg managed to catch several stripers in the Connecticut River. It was a crazy time, but by then Freedman and Wheeler were ecstatic about the possibilities for a TV show. They were very happy when they left the next day.

I had a long talk with Freedman later. To him, Greg is far more than just a fisherman. He has many different sides. "He's charismatic, there's no question," he told me. "He's very comfortable in his skin. You could see on *Shark Tank*, he just exudes confidence. And people really like him."

Freedman envisions the show being like a cross between the reality show *Duck Dynasty* and the popular 1980s and '90s NBC sitcom *Cheers*—only instead of being set in a fictional bar populated with colorful characters who come together to drink and banter with each other, the action in this show would take place in a fishing-tackle shop with Greg and his fishermen friends, who drop in to visit or help him with his work.

"I see the World Record Striper Company as Greg's headquarters . . . his base where all of his friends show up," said Freedman. "If you're a fisherman, a bait and tackle shop is a place you go to hang out, BS, buy some equipment, or just be around a community of fishermen, which are an interesting breed unto themselves."

Freedman should know: he's been an avid fisherman himself for years and spends countless hours fishing for striped bass on his boat or from the shore near his home on Long Island. "Fishing is a disease," he said, laughing. "Once you get hooked, it grabs you. It's very addictive. These guys sacrifice everything to pursue fish. That's why they're not married, or can't stay married, because when nature creates these moments when the fish are moving through, they just have to go after them."

He has nothing but admiration for Greg's skills as a fisherman. "He has almost this sixth sense—he really thinks like a fish. I consider myself a very good fisherman, but Greg is the real deal."

Freedman also likes the fact that Greg is encouraging anglers to practice catch-and-release with striped bass. "The striped bass is an absolutely adored fish—one of the most important recreational fish around," he said. "But not everyone understands the importance of releasing them. They don't understand the ecological side of it. Everyone says to me, 'Don't you want to bring home dinner?' And I say, 'No; striped bass are much too valuable to catch just once.'"

So where does this all go from here? The next step will be to do more videotaping when the stripers are here in large numbers this summer and create a pilot to shop around to television networks. If Greg's pendulum swings higher still, he may soon begin a new phase of his life—as a television celebrity.

EPILOGUE

September 16, 2017. Brewer Pilots Point Marina, Westbrook, Connecticut. The Fishing for Cancer Tournament is finally over, the barbecue has begun, and the awards for the biggest fish will soon be handed out—but not to our team. All of the huge fish—with the exception of some good-sized bluefish we caught this morning—eluded our team. But we were winners in other ways: we had raised the most money for the charity *and* the tournament was catch-and-release. It was originally going to be a kill tournament, but Greg insisted he would not lend his name to it or participate in any way unless it was strictly catch-and-release. Thanks to him, every single one of the striped bass caught in the tournament was still alive.

At the captains' meeting the previous evening, each team was given an official peel-and-stick measuring tape to paste down on the decks of our boats in a place where a fish could be quickly laid down next to it and photographed to establish its length. The tournament rules required three photos of each potential winning fish: one of the angler holding the fish, one of the fish lying next to the measuring tape, and one as the fish was being released alive.

Epilogue

Greg encouraged everyone to send an email message from their smartphones, with photos of a potential winning fish attached, to the headquarters as soon as possible after releasing the fish, so other anglers would immediately know the size of the top contender at any given time. If the biggest fish caught so far was, say, 45 inches, the bar was set, and everyone would know that they could release anything smaller without subjecting the fish to any unnecessary additional stress just to take pictures.

At the end of the meeting, everyone had headed out, hoping to catch a bigger striped bass or bluefish than anyone else. The sun was just dipping below the horizon as we entered Long Island Sound. The remnants of Hurricane Jose still lingered along the East Coast, creating huge swells and wild surf, but we barely felt it in the shelter of the sound as we blasted across the water with the throttle down, salt spray exploding over us. Greg had decided to take our boat all the way to Montauk Point, nearly thirty miles away at the easternmost tip of Long Island. Of course, it was a gamble. Montauk could be hit or miss this time of year. If the stripers are moving through in decent numbers it could be truly great—or not, if they were absent. The latter was the case that night for our boat and all the others working the waters off Montauk.

Walter Anderson and his teammates, Keith Salisbury and Ed Noble, had a much better time. They had decided to stay close to shore that evening, fishing along the Connecticut coast, and got into some stripers within fifteen minutes of leaving the marina. At one point, all three of them had fish on at the same time. When Keith landed a 46-incher, Walter took the necessary photographs and emailed them to the Fishing for Cancer headquarters. "Greg thought there was a good chance my boat would catch the first fish," said Walter. "He said to me, 'Look, if you catch a good fish early, set the bar. That'll save a lot of fish from getting manhandled.'"

On our boat, when we saw the photo, we immediately knew things were not shaping up well for us. Greg laughed and took it all in stride.

Epilogue

At another time in his life, he might have raced back to the Connecticut coast and spent the entire night working the water, determined to get the biggest bass, but his outlook had definitely matured. We continued to fish where we were for a few more hours, then we tied up in Montauk and slept on the boat. The next morning, we caught a few bluefish on the way back before calling it quits around noon, ending the tournament in good spirits.

Keith's 46-inch striper ended up in second place overall, behind a 48-incher caught by Chris Staab; however, Keith did catch a 37.75-inch bluefish, the longest one taken in the tournament. But Walter also sees Greg as a big winner. "His goal, number one, was to raise money for the charity, and number two, to make this a catch-and-release tournament," said Walter. "He achieved both goals. I told him I was proud of him."

Like Greg, Walter is adamantly opposed to killing large striped bass. "I had an experience a few years ago fishing with two friends in a two-day tournament," he said. "We came in at the end of the second day, and there must have been almost fifty fish lying dead on the docks: all these dead female striped bass. And all these guys were walking around saying, 'Anyone want this?' 'Anyone want this fish?' It was disgusting. I said to my friends, 'I will never enter another kill tournament.'"

The problem with kill tournaments is that all too often people will bring in every decent-sized fish they catch in hopes that it will be a winner. If you have thirty boats competing, you could end up with thirty huge dead bass on the dock, but only one can win.

"Why kill those fish anyway?" said Walter. "They're not as good to eat as smaller ones. A fillet on a big fish can be two inches thick. What are you going to do with that? And it also has a lot of mercury in it."

Catch-and-release makes so much sense. And ironically, the Fishing for Cancer Tournament probably raised a lot more money than it would have had it been a kill tournament. Certainly Walter and some of the other top fishermen would not have entered it otherwise.

Greg's greatest hope now is that tournaments like this will set an example that others will follow. He is determined to push tirelessly for the conservation of the striped bass.

ACKNOWLEDGMENTS

I owe a deep debt of gratitude to the many people who helped me as I worked on this book, but especially Greg Myerson, whose friendship, strength, and generosity kept me going as I struggled through the darkest time of my life. I first met him six years ago when I was taking my son Jack, a high school senior, to look at Wesleyan University, not far from where Greg lived. At first I wasn't sure if I would take on this project, writing the story of Greg's life, but after talking with him for a couple of hours I realized what a remarkable person he is, with a backstory much larger and more compelling than the fact that he caught a record-breaking striped bass.

As Jack and I drove home the next day in a blizzard, I mentally sketched out the structure of the book, eager to start working on a proposal to present to publishers. I had no way of knowing that this would be the last trip my son and I would ever take together. Barely three months later, my wife and I and our three daughters faced the most devastating tragedy of our lives. Jack was dead—and worse, he had taken his own life. Sorrow hung over us like a dense shroud for months as we teetered at the edge of despair with no end in sight.

Acknowledgments

One of the first things I did was to call Greg and say I would not be able to write this book. Indeed, I doubted I would ever write anything again. I told him he would have no trouble finding someone else to take over the project. But Greg wouldn't hear of it. He said I was the only person he wanted to write his story. "Take five years, six years, as long as you want," he said. "And you can dedicate the book to Jack."

Greg once told me that I had saved his life when I drove him to a hospital emergency room late one night. But really, it was Greg who saved my life. He picked me up from the ground in my moment of deepest desolation and kept me going. Without his help, I know I would never have written this or any other future books, and for that I am eternally grateful.

I also thank everyone who allowed me to interview them, including many of Greg's family members and friends—especially Walter Anderson and Stephen Hoag. And I thank everyone at Houghton Mifflin Harcourt who helped me with this book, especially executive editor Lisa White, who also worked with me on two previous books, *The Grail Bird* and *Falcon Fever,* and is a good friend. I am indebted to my literary agent, Russ Galen, for his expert advice throughout this project and also for being the person who first told me about Greg and set up our introduction.

Above all, I thank my wife, Rachel Dickinson—an author herself, who read early drafts of the book and offered solid advice and encouragement—and my daughters, Railey, Clara, and Gwen. Without their support, none of this would have been possible.